E
& Leaves

The open-minded guide to English

Nicholas Waters

International Waters

Special edition
Published in England, 9th November 2006 by
International Waters

ISBN 1-90533601-2

A CIP catalogue number is available from the
British Library

Printed and bound in England by
TJ International, Padstow, Cornwall.
Cover layout: Graphics One, Norwich

International Waters
Norwich, England. Växjö, Sweden

www.eatsrootsandleaves.co.uk

So, what's it all about?

This book is not a style manual. It is not a call to arms. It is not even a call to hands, fingers or even pens. *Eats Roots & Leaves* is a cry for freedom!

Almost every single day there is a letter in a newspaper complaining about the decline of the English language. If we believe these writers, English is being abused by people who don't know the rules and debased by the media who should know better. Errant apostrophes, inappropriate vocabulary and the accusation that young people no longer speak and write properly are just the tip of the icecube. Moans about mixed metaphors and alliteration are also reaching a crescendo[1].

The pedants who criticise "mistakes" in other people's English are often mistaken themselves. They point out miniscule and often irrelevant errors while ignoring the greater purpose of language: communication. I accuse them of being grammar fascists. I suppose that I should really use a term like lingua fascist or perhaps even lingo fascist. This is because *Eats, Roots & Leaves* looks at many more aspects of English than just grammar. It would be pedantic and very sad to concentrate on the absence, or misplacing, of a few soggy apostrophes.

English is the bastard child of the Anglo-Saxons and the Normans, influenced in infancy by Viking relatives and brought up by foster parents well versed in Latin. The result of this is the

[1] Before you protest, please be patient. There is an explanation in chapter 8.

complicated, confused and sometimes contradictory language that we use today.

As society has changed, English has developed novel ways of expression, new terms have arisen and words have changed their meanings. The grammar fascists, who seem to reject much of what is modern about English, would like to turn the clock back to a mythical year zero. They would dictate language rules to be set in stone forever. However, some so-called rules have no place in our language. Those annoying little irrelevancies are there simply on the decree of some self-appointed style gurus a long time ago. Speaking and writing any language is not a case of 'I've learnt it and that is it.' It is a life-long learning process.

The great strength of English is adaptability and flexibility. There has never been a master plan for the development of English. Instead, the language has developed by organic means with people speaking and writing as they see fit. English has prospered by common agreement despite, or possibly because of, the absence of legislation or official designation. There is no authority that lays down the laws concerning how English should be. No-one owns the language, although it belongs to everyone. We have choices about how to use OUR language. *Eats Roots & Leaves* is pro-choice.

Eats, Roots & Leaves reclaims English from the *Perfectors*. These are grammar fascists who dedicate their lives to the pursuit of some form of language nirvana. A state of absolute perfection in English does not exist. It never has and never will outside of a few deluded minds. Being a writer is supposed to be a lonely profession. The pedants are the lonely ones, their eyes and minds closed to inevitable change in language. I certainly haven't been lonely writing this book. Over the last eight years, I have been out and about, up hill and down dale and around the block a couple of times following a trail of authentic English. Even the title, *Eats, Roots & Leaves*, came from a chance encounter with English on the other side of the world. This book exposes the sad lives of those who seek to subjugate the English language to their own rules.

Eats, Roots & Leaves is not a textbook. It does not prescribe what is absolutely correct and therefore preach that everything else in comparison must be unacceptable. I believe that you can make up your own mind. There are, after all, plenty of good reference works out there to look up individual points of grammar.

Eats, Roots & Leaves does aim to raise the level of awareness and debate. There are fewer instances in English than you might think where we can say with absolute certainty what is right or wrong. There are so many different contexts and situations where English is used that allow flexibility in our choices of vocabulary, syntax, punctuation and pronunciation.

Many of the rants from grammar fascists are petty, insignificant and often irrelevant. What is important is not to be slaves to imaginary rules, but to encourage people to express themselves.

This book does have a message: Do not be afraid of change. Instead, welcome and embrace it. English is a vibrant living language that is thriving precisely because of its propensity to adapt to the ever-changing needs of society. Language should be enjoyed which is obvious from its two functions:

1. a means of communication.

2. a wonderful game to be played where words can be manipulated and mangled, speech used imaginatively and expressions created and parodied.

The two functions are equally important.

So please, set your irony filter to its lowest setting and read with an open mind. The only intolerance you will find is to the grammar fascists who advocate zero tolerance.

I have written this foreword to classify *Eats, Roots & Leaves* so that the bookshop knows where to place it on the shelves, a potential buyer should be able to find it and eventually the jumble sale organiser will know which pile to put it in.

Norwich
September 2006

This book is dedicated to all the hard-working and long-suffering English teachers in Sweden.

A cautionary note

There may well be inconsistencies and oddities of language in this book. I know that there are. Some have been deliberately planted. Having read this far, you may have noticed some already.

In this collection of discourses concerning the English language, I have invented some new words. The first time that they are presented, they are shown in italics and begin with capital letters.

I have also used italics to denote examples and for the names of books, newspapers and the like. Quotation marks are reserved for quotations!

Some errors that may have slipped through are a result of my ignorance or my rejection of the advice of my excellent proof-reader. If you find something that you don't like or disagree with, please let me know. The website is an excellent point of contact.

However, I will not apologise for taking liberties with the language. I strive to reach a good standard of communication, without falling into the traps that the grammar fascists have set. Henry Ford reputedly said: The man who never made mistakes, never made anything. I can a Ford to make miss steaks as I am not setting myself up as a *Perfector*.

Contents

1. J'accuse!

Integrity without knowledge is weak and useless, and knowledge without integrity is dangerous and dreadful.

Samuel Johnson

One of my earliest recollections of newspapers concerns the letters pages of the national dailies. I used to get up at around 5 o'clock in the morning, six days a week, to deliver the papers. For 7 years, I worked for a small shop, long since taken over by a national chain, called Yards. In the summer when it was lighter and warmer, I usually did two rounds, but in winter I had only my regular route. I arrived just as early at the paper shop though and had a chance to peruse the papers while Mr Billet would put them in order for the 21 boys and one girl who would deliver them before school. From the first day, the correspondence captured my attention in a way that the headlines usually failed to do. People often wrote under pseudonyms and, I discovered over a period of time, that there seemed to be a scale which indicated the degree of outrage of the correspondents; disappointed, disgruntled, disgusted, etc. What struck me was how often the letters referred to the English language going downhill. I became interested in the subject and began to wonder what kind of person is moved to put pen to Basildon Bond or paper in typewriter.

The level of correspondence bemoaning the decline of English does not seem to have abated over the years; in fact I wonder if the opposite isn't true. I have grown up and no longer deliver newspapers. The 'Exasperateds of Exeter' and 'Bemuseds of Basingstoke' that I remember from my youth must surely have passed on to a better place where misplaced apostrophes trouble them no more. So they ought to be a dying breed. Or could it be that at a certain age, rather like we can become more susceptible to diabetes, there is a creeping indignation that compels people to complain about the misuse of language? Perhaps 'Disgusted of Tunbridge Wells' has been cloned and carbon copies (there are people still using carbon paper. It is still on sale.) are scattered around the country. Was there a time, in some way better than today, when people talked properly and respected the written word? There is certainly quite a number that seem to want to hark back to a past when everyone spoke properly, spelled perfectly, wrote prosaically without error and wish to lecture the rest of us about how bad our English is. These people, who might be content to be called sticklers and pedants, I label *Grammar Fascists*.

I use what might seem like a rather extreme term because of the way that the grammar fascists behave. Their actions are purely negative. They are not trying to improve what they see as a lack of knowledge and understanding about how English should be used. Rather, they want to highlight what they believe to be errors and then to point accusing fingers and apportion blame. They have no interest in people bettering themselves linguistically. Their joy is simply in the exposure of others' mistakes and heaping ridicule upon the perpetrators. Their true delight, which must be un-British as English originally had no word for it, is *shadenfreude* - taking pleasure in the misfortune of others. Fascist is not too strong a word to describe such people.

Unlike other kinds of fascists - who form parties, march in the streets, parade banners and dress up in fancy uniforms - grammar fascists shun the idea of any collective or overtly public form of action. Instead they resort to more insidious ways to get their views across. Ordinary fascists simply want to take over society to save us all from a depraved and corrupt democracy. Grammar fascists don't need to take over, because they believe that they already own the system and that all they have to do is to snipe from the sidelines and keep everyone in line. Of course, the biggest difference between a common or garden fascist and that of the grammar variety is that the latter is single-minded in fighting the good fight over language. The term grammar fascist covers a multitude of malcontents. Some might simply utter a 'tut, tut,' while others will scream 'zero tolerance.' The only thing that unites them is their diversity. Grammar fascism is probably best represented as being like a series of cults, each one having a special belief system.

One very vocal group is the *Apostropharians*. They believe that the biggest threat to modern society is the misplaced use of the genitive apostrophe. The members of this cult worship punctuation and have a particular fetish for a grubby little ink spot. Apostropharians think that being unable to use the apostrophe in the ways that they approve reveals the full extent to which education is failing and the country is going to the dogs. According to them, we will soon descend into the kind anarchy where market stallholders can describe their fruit and veg without paying the slightest bit of notice to the grammar book. Chapter 10 is devoted to their exploits.

A quite different sect is called the *Nuancers*. These people are dedicated to maintaining the difference in meanings of pairs of words that seem to be blending in modern society, word pairs such as *infer* and *imply*. The nuancers are one of the oldest factions and venerate the distinctions which they regard as holy and sacrosanct. You can meet them in chapter 8.

A further group is the *Little Englanders*. It might be unfair to imply (or infer) that this is a bunch of retired colonels and people who won't touch *The Independent* or *The Guardian* as they are not proper broadsheets anymore. The Little Englanders see an invisible enemy massing its troops offshore to take over this sceptred isle. This perceived foe is attempting to undo the lasting legacy of the British Empire. They are, of course, referring to the Americans. The Yanks are bombarding us with movies, Cheers and Friends and, worst of all, the computer geeks with their *colors* and *programs*. British is doomed to a future of becoming a downsized language that is little more than a dialect of CNN and Hollywood. And that is so not acceptable! Chapters 15 and 16 record the fallacy of their arguments.

Even within these groups there are factions. For example the apostropharians are deeply split. First there are the *Fundamentalists*. This is a small clique of men, usually geographically located in the outer Home Counties, who would legislate to make infringements against the language a criminal offence. They would also insist on English being the official language and set minimum standards of spelling, punctuation, grammar and even pronunciation. Violators would be sent to a penitentiary. Here the offenders would serve their penance with pens. Release being conditional on meeting the standard laid down by a new Ministry of Expression. The fundamentalists would punish even the slightest deviance from what they see as acceptable grammar. Until the glorious day comes when their aims are enshrined in law, they have two main weapons. The first is ridicule. They heap waves of derision on those who either don't know better or who do, but are seen as sloppy and ill-disciplined. The second weapon is to blame society, the education system, teachers and indeed anyone who hasn't mastered (see how sexist the language is) English as well as they. The fundamentalists, however, are continually troubled by splinter groups which disagree as to how the revolution should be carried out.

The *Penists* have difficulty coming to terms with modern technology. A typewriter is about the latest technological advance that they might allow. Being a mechanical device, it has none of the tricks of a computer keyboard or a mobile phone touchpad. The internet is for ignorant people who have never read a good book. Spellcheckers and word processing programmes are for the lazy, slovenly and un-learned masses (by the way, grammar fascists love words where the *-ed* sound is pronounced, I'm not sure why, but probably because it doesn't sound modern).

The more extreme *Quillists* seek a return to their year zero: 1616. It is from this time that they believe English started its decline. This was the year of the death of Shakespeare. Quillists are easy to spot. They greet each other with phrases such as 'Hail, good fellow' and 'well met.' They are a weird bunch who inhabit the modern world but imagine bygone days. Sadly, they honestly believe that people actually spoke to each other as if they were characters in a Shakespeare play. April 23rd is the best day for quillist spotting. This is the holiest day in their calendar being the supposed date both of the Bard's birth and his demise. This is also the day of pilgrimage to Stratford-upon-Avon, although would-be quillists can be seen all-year-round on the South Bank in London.

By far the largest of the factions is the *Orthodox*. These are the letter writers to which I allude in the opening paragraph. They seek, by ceaseless lobbying and campaigning, to turn around the moral decline of the language by pointing out the errors of our ways and offering a picture of a new linguistic Jerusalem in England's green and pleasant land. This heaven on earth would have a system whereby anyone using punctuation incorrectly would be rehabilitated by attending Sunday school to re-learn from the scriptures of the holy grammar books.

Finally, there is the *Provisional Wing*. This loose organisation consists of a number of cells, each with one or more members, with information passed on a need-to-know basis. They are only concerned with direct action to stem the flow of sloppy English in public. Operating often under cover of darkness, the provisionals undertake missions armed to the teeth with industrial-sized buckets of Tippex and marker pens. They target the non-food sections of supermarkets, posters on railway stations and council notices. Mercilessly correcting as they go, darting from shadow to shadow, the shock troops of the movement abhor the failure of orthodoxy to achieve progress and believe that society at large must be brought to book through militant action. Aberrant apostrophes are whited-out and deficiencies in punctuation penned in. Some of these extremists even have sheets of printed apostrophes on sticky paper to carry around and distribute. Can you believe anyone could be so dedicated and petty at the same time? Could this illustrate the true meaning of the word *stickler*?

There is, however, one factor that unites grammar fascism: indignation. Whether they thunder or are flabbergasted, grammar fascists share a sense that things are not as they should be and that something has to be done.

So far, I have only scratched the surface as there are so many types of grammar fascism.

Because of the much splintered nature of the movement and for the sake of simplicity, I shall refer generically to the term grammar fascist. I shall return to the particular foibles of certain sects in later chapters. Are these people dangerous or just harmless cranks? Do Special Branch and MI5 monitor the activities of the self-appointed language police? Usually the security forces would invent a word for the target of their observations. We will have to wait until the archives are opened in 50 years to find out what that word is. If the spy world hasn't come up with a new word, let me provide one. The term for an individual grammar fascist is *Gramfa*.

Finding a gramfa is not difficult. All you need to do is to take a look at the letters pages in the national press. I wish to share with you a few of my favourites. I have changed the names to avoid embarrassment, but I give my oath that the letters are genuine.

Wrong date

Sir: congratulations on correctly designating the date 11/9. Many refer to 9/11, but I am unaware of any significant event that occurred on 9 November.
I B Smith
London NW1

This particular person seems unable to accept that 9/11 has passed into the language as a proper noun. A linguistic result of the events of that infamous September day in 2001 is that we now all know that the Americans put the month before the day when writing dates. Perhaps he is a Little Englander, fearing a bit of *Amerocreep* in British English. Saying or writing 9/11 does not mean accepting the American way of writing the date. It was their event so they have a right to name it. Get over it buddy!

This is my favouritest example of grammar fascism.
This is the first sentence of a letter in *The
Independent*.

**Sir: having been fighting the
misuse of "decimate" for
something like 50 years...**
Arthur Campbell
Edinburgh

What a wonderful life this person must have! I
would have thought that after 50 years Mr
Campbell ought to have retired. I wonder if it was a
full-time job and if so, who paid his wages.

What the correspondent from Scotland is
complaining about is that the modern sense of
decimate is destroy or at least very badly damage.
Originally it meant to reduce by a tenth. From my
Latin lessons at school, I understood that the
Roman legions were quite intolerant of failure. A
Roman army defeated in battle would be punished
by one tenth of the legionnaires being put to death.
That is, the legion was decimated. This concept was
not a general feature of armies in later years, not
even in the so-called dark ages. The word, however,
did not disappear and through time acquired its
current generally understood meaning. Is the
language any poorer because we have a different
concept of failure and don't execute people for
messing up?

You can find grammar fascists almost
anywhere. A fine example of someone pre-occupied
with language comes from a conversation between
two people that I had the pleasure to work with at

a little-known educational establishment. Following a summer holiday where it had been possible to catch up with some reading, a colleague wandered into the office of the pedant-in-chief of the university. She spotted a paperback book on his desk and asked: "What did you think of the book?" His reply was: "She puts her adverbs in strange places." You or I might have given a précis of the plot or a comment on the characters. But this man showed such a pre-occupation with the details of grammar that you have to wonder if he could get any enjoyment from reading at all. But then happiness is not an abundant commodity in the world of pedants. Indeed, the main purpose of a grammar fascist is to be a killjoy. They want to spread gloom and despondency while demoralising the nation with constant gripes about the state of English

This could have been another example of grammar fascism, this time edited, and again from the letters page of *The Independent*.

Wash your hands

Sir: with reference to the news that "one third of kitchen workers do not wash their hands after using the lavatory".   ... After visiting the toilet I usually wash my hands in the lavatory itself ... a lavatory is a wash-hand basin not a water closet.
Dr Munroe Law
Edinburgh

Dr Law is quite correct. Look in your own dictionary to check if you wish. This isn't grammar fascism (at least I hope it isn't). What I believe he is pointing out is that common usage has caused a change in the use of lavatory. The word comes from a Latin verb meaning to wash, but the vast majority of people think of a lavatory as another word for toilet. It doesn't matter how a dictionary defines a word, its true meaning lies in what people in general understand it to mean. So we mustn't hasten to harshly judge what might, at first sight, appear to be a nuancer. As you already know, grammar fascists are quick to judge and condemn. I have no intention of doing likewise and I will give Dr Law the benefit of any perceivable doubt. But there is something nagging at my mind. Why do doctors have to make sure that everyone else knows that they are a doctor? Surely it's not to show some superiority to those who are not doctors? And rarely do the good doctors tell us in what field they qualified as a doctor. Maybe Dr Law is a doctor in inter-urinal physics and therefore qualified to lecture us on the subject? Oh, and, one other thing. I mentioned earlier in this chapter about the fragmented nature of grammar fascism. In highlighting one area of the language, Dr Law has inadvertently attacked a quite different, but nonetheless strongly held grammar fascist belief. You'll find out what it is in chapter 16.

Another, much milder kind of language fascism comes from pointing out obvious double meanings. Instructions on supermarket shelves such as 'Customers are advised to wash fruit before eating' get the grammar fascists muttering, 'Why do I have wash some fruit before every meal that I eat?' They are forgetting the ellipsis (leaving words out) that is totally acceptable to them in newspaper headlines, but not on signs. What was meant was 'Customers are advised to wash fruit before eating it.' The missing word which allowed the double meaning was *it*. However, putting *it* at the end appears inferior to the sentence without it. *It* is a word that fosters unease. A good number of people confuse *it's* and *its*. Many more are sure that there are rules about when and how to use *it*, but are equally unsure about what those rules might be. An old adage comes to mind: 'If in doubt, leave it out.' So, rather than risk making a mistake and incur the wrath of the perfectors, the supermarket marketers have actually given the tut-tut brigade their chance to murmur discontentedly. *Eats Roots & Leaves* will revisit supermarkets in later chapters.

Of course it is not only letter writers and miscellaneous doctors that are prone to finding fault. There are a number of books that tackle the tricky area of errors. One such tome has the title: *A How-Not-To Guide to the 47 Most Common Mistakes in English Made by Journalists, Broadcasters, and Others Who Should Know Better.* Grammar fascists buy certain books neither to engage in any discussion about language nor to see things from a different perspective. They read certain works only to get their prejudices about supposed language decay confirmed.

Quite understandably, grammar fascists do not feel flattered by this epithet. Many prefer to describe themselves as sticklers. I looked up stickler in a number of dictionaries. Here is one example:

stickler noun (usually a stickler for something) someone who fastidiously insists on something. Etymology: Anglo-Saxon *stihtan* to set in order.

What then, I wonder, is the difference between sticklerism and fascism? Because whichever name you choose, a fanatic is someone who can't change their mind and won't change the subject. In my favourite dictionary, *The Macquarie*, the definition was very similar. The exception being that fastidious was replaced by *unyielding*. My point exactly! Grammar fascists are intransigent. They are saying to us 'talk to the hand, because the face ain't listening.' They do not and will not listen to any other viewpoint. I think that I shall be a stickler on this point and continue to use the term *grammar fascist*.

2. The pedant's way

There is no original truth, only original error.

Gaston Bachelard

Pedants Way ought to be a rather ordinary cul-de-sac somewhere in Surrey between Guildford and Reigate. Many inhabitants of this commuter belt countryside take the train up to London. Thus they have between 45 minutes and an hour (depending on the right type of leaves having fallen) to do their crosswords and read the letters page. The travellers may even have time to compose a mental missive of their own, highlighting the terrible propensity of young people to write *he/she* or, worse, *they* in order not to assume the masculine form. The letter will most often be entitled: 'It's political correctness gone mad.' For this is the true pedant's way. No, not the railway line, but a belief that English is going to the dogs. But where did these sticklers get their ideas from?

The story of grammar fascism really begins in the 1700s with a fellow called Robert Lowth. In those days there was a rather pleasant custom for graduates of Oxford and Cambridge. A degree from either of these two universities would provide a meal ticket for life. If they couldn't think of anything else to do, graduates would usually be fixed up with a nice little job in the Church of England. Lowth followed this career path and like many contemporaries got a salary, a house and a parish. However, not content with being a country parson he also became a professor of poetry at

Oxford. Perhaps he missed the church, so he went back to being a vicar, was appointed bishop of St David's in 1766 and subsequently occupied the bishoprics of Oxford and then London. Rumour had it that he was even offered the post of Archbishop of Canterbury. So, quite a career man was Robert Lowth. His appearance in this book is due to the publication in 1762 of *A Short Introduction to English Grammar*.

Why Lowth didn't confine himself to preaching and poetry, God only knows. But he felt the need to write a grammar book. Maybe he did it because it was the in thing to do. Between 1750 and 1800 more than 200 works on grammar and language were published. Samuel Johnson had published his famous dictionary in 1755 and now, having sorted out the meanings of words, it was time to fix the grammar. When dealing with grammar there is always a bit of a dilemma. Do you simply describe the way that people use language or do you also determine in what way language should be used? These are called the descriptive and prescriptive approaches, respectively. A descriptive approach looks at usage, distribution and history rather than correctness. A prescriptive approach, on the other hand, would rule on rationality, historical grammatical usage or conformity to some or other standard.

Most previous writing on grammar had been descriptive. Lowth's grammar followed the pattern. However, if we look at the full title of the book, *A Short Introduction to English Grammar with Critical Notes*, we might get a clue as to what lies within. Lowth had the intention to "lay down

23

rules", and "beside shewing what is right ... pointing out what is wrong."

So, his grammar marks the true commencement of the prescriptive line. For example, he wrote in a footnote: "Whose is by some authors made the Possessive Case of which, and applied to things as well as persons; I think, improperly." Kindly note that he wrote *I think*. Lowth was expressing an opinion, a preference.

Lowth's method included criticising what he called "false syntax." He chose examples from Milton, Shakespeare, Swift and other famous writers. He even picked on the *King James Bible*.

I'm sure almost anyone could, should they care to do so, find instances of unusual grammar and punctuation and strange words in any great work of literature. After all, every author has the right to be wrong and this right is equal to, or greater than, the responsibility to be correct. But Lowth started from an unusual angle. His approach was based largely on Latin grammar. He made his pronouncements based on an attempt to superimpose Latin grammar onto English. This is odd enough, but it actually went against his own stated principle as Lowth condemned "forcing the English under the rules of a foreign Language." Thus Lowth not only formalised grammar fascism, but he also became the first grammar hypocrite.

Some of Lowth's linguistic sermons are still with us today. The most infamous of them all was his decree against ending sentences with a preposition. Lowth didn't invent this rule, but he was responsible for spreading it far and wide. Lowth certainly didn't like the line in

Shakespeare's *As you like it* that reads: "Who do you speak to?" Lowth would have written "To whom do you speak?" At the same time, he also opened up the everlasting *who versus whom* can of worms. But why did he do this? More importantly, by what authority did he make these judgements? Quite simply, it was his own personal taste and therefore no other power need be consulted.

Jeremy Bentham invented the concept of *ipsedixitism*. He said that all unsupported assertions were the result of conviction alone and therefore invalid. So when someone begins a sentence: "Trust me..." we should consider thinking exactly the opposite! *Ipse dixit* means *he himself said it*. The only basis for accepting a statement then rests on the credibility of the speaker. If you sell enough copies, maybe people will believe it. Lowth certainly sold enough copies. If you tell a lie big enough and keep repeating it, people will eventually come to believe it. Proof of this can be found in the origin of that very statement. So many people have attributed this idea to Hitler's propaganda minister, Joseph Goebbels. While he undoubtedly said it, he wasn't the first. This particular fascist was, however, a plagiarist. He got the idea from Lenin: "A lie told often enough becomes truth." But the lie about the origin of the saying has been told so often that most people think that it was the nasty Nazi that made it up. Those who quote grammar chapter and verse may well be guilty of ipsedixitism. They give no supporting arguments and attempt to give the impression that they are speaking about universal truths. This, in a nutshell, sums up Robert Lowth and his approach to grammar. He even quoted himself in giving an example.

Next on the scene comes Lindley Murray, a Quaker born in America. According to most biographies, Murray had been a successful lawyer and businessman in New York. For reasons of ill-health, he retired to the Yorkshire village of Holgate around 1784. However, one important fact is often excluded. Murray was a Loyalist. In fact he fled the newly-formed United States after the Declaration of Independence and subsequent war, which his side lost. While at Holgate, he wrote his own *English Grammar*. His aim was to make an easy grammar for the benefit of the learner. He admitted in the introduction that he was doing little more than taking what he regarded as the best bits of other people's work. Murray borrowed extensively from Robert Lowth and Thomas Sheridan. So he ended up regurgitating Lowth's grammar rules. What was it that Lenin said? Murray did, however, introduce the concept of logic and it was this kind of thinking that resulted in the prohibition of the double negative. There is a look at this idea in chapter 7. Another consequence of Murryan logic was that the interdict against the split infinitive came about during the late 1700s as did the rules about *shall* and *will*. Murray has been called the 'father of English grammar' but I have yet to find out who said this originally. But someone obviously liked him enough to say so. During this boom time for the grammar industry, Murray wrote 11 school textbooks and sold over 20 million copies. Using only the work of "best writers" to set his "standard", Murray's best seller was the

English Reader. Abraham Lincoln described the *English Reader* as "the best schoolbook ever put in the hands of an American youth." The *English Reader* was the standard work in American for more than a generation. Even Lenin didn't manage that kind of influence and he controlled a whole country!

Quickly passing over 2 centuries of grammar fascism, it is sufficient to say that the advent of popular newspapers and universal education in the western world did a great deal to concretise the teachings of the 18th century dogmatists. In the study of logic there is a concept called *argumentum ad numerum*. In plain words, something is proven true on the grounds that many or all people believe it. If everybody believes in something, then it is so. This is what the grammar fascists have relied upon for many years. The educated and governing classes accepted and propagated standardised versions of English. Thus, they have been able to ensure these Lowthian and Murryan 'principles' have been accepted as right and proper because there has been so little dissent during the last two hundred years. Style guides became popular towards the end of the last millennium. While many had the noble aim of encouraging clarity of expression, these style guides attempted to dictate where they should advise. Not surprising then, that in the early 21st century there are still grammar fascists.

Just as a bit of fun and to give you a better idea of the kind of person who might attend the Church of the Latter Day Sages, let us invent an imaginary grammar fascist. First, this person should have a name, so what about Chris? Surname: Woodhead. Occupation: Former inspector of schools, now working for a private university. Main grouses about language: 'Everything is someone else's fault and this wouldn't happen if state schools were abolished and everyone had private education, except we need those corduroy-wearing, bearded, lefty state school teachers to heap the blame on and give me well-paid spots as an "expert" on TV and radio. Oops, now I've put two *ands* in one sentence, but this isn't going out live is it? So we can edit it out later. I wouldn't want anyone to think that *I* was less than perfect.' Let's imagine one of those lucrative radio appearances (!) where the grammar (optional word in this case) fascist speaks. To create a sense of realism, let's say it was on 7th September 2005 at around 09.24 am and the fictional, Mr Woodhead (with no allusions to the main substance inside his head) is talking about the English language. On grammar we shall have him say: "This is an issue that we should confront more sternly than we are" On texting he might say something like: "This is pollution in the language." Of course no-one in their right mind would actually say such things. You see, grammar fascists are people for whom learning grammar is far more important than communicating. The use of the word *confront* gives us a clue as to the kind of character that people have to deal with.

The point is we don't need to invent people like this. We have already seen genuine examples from newspapers. Grammar fascists pop up like toast in the sound and visual media too. One of the presenters of the Radio 4 *Today* programme was hired for a recent BBC TV show about the English language. His role was to provide comment as a professional user of the language. He was asked by Anne Robinson: "John, what do you think of text messages?" His reply was: "I detes...well...I don't have a mobile." He added: "I think it's rubbish." The man is making a judgement without the experience of actually using a mobile phone. Anyone with a teenage daughter who communicates by sending truncated messages with no capitalisation, abbreviated words, letters replaced by numbers and a complete absence of punctuation would experience a very rapid learning curve. Initial disgust would be replaced by expediency. One quickly comes to realise that the thumb tribes are so called because some teenagers send huge numbers of texts. Although these youngsters quickly develop oversized muscles at the base of the right thumb, there is a need to rattle off replies quickly. This means that the language is adapted, reduced to the minimum and employs phonetic spellings to save on characters, time and effort. I have sent the person in question a copy of this book; I do hope that he reads chapter 12. You have to know what you are talking about before you can pass judgement. Please, no ipsedixitism, MR H.

I shall leave this gentle stroll down the pedants way with an example of a grammar fascist who himself does not know the rules. This is a short extract from a very long and otherwise dull diatribe posted on an internet message board by someone using the name *carl31* on April 20th, 2006 at 12:12. Complaining about a previous poster, Carl lets fly:

People in glass houses shouldn't throw stones. Is that how you usually spell "absolutley"? Your grammar leaves a lot to be desired. The third word in the post is "it's" meaning 'belonging to it'. The short version of "it is" should read "its". Entering the world of clichés Carl should be asked to take a test. Make these words into a grammatically correct sentence: Pot, kettle, black, calling the.

3. Britannia waives the rules

There are no rules here; we're trying to accomplish something.

Thomas Alva Edison

Please put your hand up if you learnt this mantra at school: 'i before e, except after c.' But don't do it if you are sat on a train or in any other public place reading this book. I meant metaphorically as in the phrase 'well, we can all put our hands up to that' although not as *putting ones hands up to something* means admitting guilt. I expect most people have heard this nice little spelling rule. That's why words like *field* are spelt *i* before *e* and words like *receipt* are spelt with those two letters the other way around. *Except after c,* of course, is one of those exceptions that proves the rule. This is a daft piece of non-logic in itself. If there is an exception, then the rule cannot a rule. 'Well, officer I always drive at 69.9 mph on the motorway. I only drove at 120 just then to prove my rule.' But what about words like *their* and *weir*. The *i* does not follow the *e* and there is no *c* anywhere to be seen. Perhaps we need to re-write this 'rule' to read "i before e, except after c, except where it doesn't!" It can only help to strengthen the case that now the exception to the exception proves the rule. 'Yes, officer that explains why I suddenly accelerated from 120 to 135.' 'Thank you, Sir. That all seems in order, sorry to trouble you. Drive safely.' I think it better to stop trying to explain each and everything in language with rules and think instead of guidelines for English. Rules are for the guidance of the wise and the obedience of the foolish

Many years ago, Miss Barrington had given over charge of her fourth year class (year six in current nomenclature) to a student teacher at Hillbourne Junior (now Middle) School. In an effort to improve spelling and get the pupils to use a dictionary, the student told us that every word had to contain at least one vowel. 'Uh?' We awoke. 'There are only five vowels and twenty-one consonants. There must be some words without vowels.' Challenged by the class response she dared us to find a word that didn't have a vowel. Dictionaries were issued. So confident was the stand-in teacher that she promised a KitKat to the first pupil to come up with a vowel-free word. I cracked it. I found the word *sty*. Then came a flood; *cry*, *my*, *try* and *fly*. I went to claim the KitKat. The response was along the lines of 'Aaaaaah. You see the *y* sounds like an *i*. So, as it takes the place of the vowel, it is a vowel.' I countered by pointing out that we had been told that letters all had names and sounds. A consonant needs a vowel to say its name: "wuh-I. *Y* needs the *i* to say its name." No KitKat appeared at the next, or any subsequent, lesson but neither did Miss Jones. In hindsight, I could say that I had encountered my first grammar fascist, but I actually discovered three things. That starting out in any job is difficult, especially one that involves having 30 smart-arsed kids like us. That you should make sure of your facts before making definitive statements. Most importantly, let the one who is without fault cast the first stone.

I used to accept that one shouldn't end a sentence with a preposition, but never understood the reason. Winston Churchill once replied to a memo where the writer had gone to great lengths not to end a sentence with a preposition. Churchill wrote: "This is the sort of English up with which I will not put." The rule is artificial and propagated by Robert Lowth simply because he decided that he knew best. Churchill's reply is a kind of hypercorrection. But there are other types too. When the rules are threatened grammar fascists mangle sentences to avoid a preposition at the end of a phrase. But so do ordinary folk trying to avoid making a mistake.

We were also taught at school not to say things like, 'me and you went London.' Instead we were advised to say, 'you and I.' This results in people saying the strangest of things because they want to avoid saying *me*. 'Pat and myself went to London' and 'Pat likes myself better than Chris.' Having internalised the *you and I* concept, the tendency is to apply it universally. This is the big problem with rules. The idea of a rule is to adhere to it rather than break it. So we go to great lengths to avoid saying what we believe to be wrong such as, 'the teacher gave a KitKat to you and I' instead of the correct 'the teacher gave a KitKat to you and me.' In answer to the question: 'Who's there?' a grammar fascist may answer: 'It is I.' Most people would probably answer: 'It's me.' I do not care to go into the rights and wrongs of this issue. I could present a case for either response. I favour the latter but would not discriminate against anyone that used the alternative. I ask those who favour *it*

is I not to criticise or try to correct the me-sayers.
Thank you.

There are some zealots who want to blame everything on schools and on one factor in particular. A BBC infotainment show called Test the Nation had language as one of its themes in 2005. The host, Anne Robinson asked: "So, is it the teachers who are to blame?" John Humphrys saved himself from being put in the same class as the wooden-headed one from the first chapter with the answer: "I daren't say that. I might meet one, one day." You undoubtedly will. The complaint is that children in schools don't learn grammar today. This suggestion is ridiculous; you cannot learn a language without grammar. The complaint arises because some people would like to see a quiz-style knowledge of grammar facts. They would like to turn the educational clock back and return to parsing, i.e. putting words into categories (verb, noun, adjective etc.) and describing the function of each word in a given sentence. What children learn today is that grammar is an integrated concept where "correctness" is relative to context. Students are encouraged to look for patterns in English rather than rote learning about word classes and form. This fosters creativity and children are encouraged to discover that language should be fun. If we were interested only in communicating facts there wouldn't be any poetry, and if there isn't poetry in language it's dull and dead. Chaucer knew it. Shakespeare practised it. That's what made them both great. Without experimentation we would never know that the borrowgroves were all mimsy at the beginning of Jabberwocky, the clocks would not have struck 13 in *Nineteen-eighty four* and the poor old *Jumblies* would never have set to sea in that sieve. A wop-bop-a-loo-bam-a lop-bam boom!

A grammar fascist called Barry Turner wrote a short piece in the *Writer's Handbook 2004* called "The Rise and Fall of English." He said: "The culprits are many and varied. The rot set in early in the 1960s when schools adopted a libertarian approach to education which involved giving up on difficult subjects including grammar." Turner has obviously not set foot in a school since about the early 1960s. Grammar fascists have opinions about language that they then transpose to a view on society. Football hooligans, ASBOs, teenage pregnancies and general bad manners are all down to the fact that youngsters today can't punctuate a sentence properly. This view might be a result of reading too many letters columns and not getting out very much.

Instead of sniping from the sidelines, why don't grammar fascists volunteer as classroom assistants in schools, help with literary programmes or at least donate money to buy books for the school library? Don't criticise, do something!

4. Dedicated Followers of Fashion

An old error is always more popular than a new truth.

German proverb

This book could have been called *Eats, Routes & Leaves*. In order to understand how we arrived at Gobbledegook Central we need to look at the history of English. Let us take the blue line on the Language Underground, stopping off at some of the significant points in the history of the language.

It is not possible to pinpoint when English started. A new language was introduced to the British Isles by the Anglo-Saxons and the Celtic languages of England were quickly replaced. Old English was written using runes, similar to those used by the Vikings and was quite different to today's language. Few examples of runes survive so that the historical evidence is scant. When Christian missionaries arrived around the year 600, they introduced the Roman alphabet and started keeping written records. The language of the missionaries was Latin and it was only after the translations ordered by Alfred the Great that there is any lasting legacy of written English. Alfred's language was inflected, that is, the function of a word is determined by the ending. Nowadays this job is done by the position in the sentence. The arrival of the Vikings had some influence on English. The language of the Norsemen was similar to Old English so that integration of new words and hybridisation was almost seamless.

When the Normans gained power in England after 1066, governing the country was made more difficult by the language barrier. Although the Normans were descendants of Viking invaders, they had rapidly integrated into the society of what is now northern France and had abandoned their Nordic language in favour of French. The conquerors spoke a very different tongue to the conquered. For almost two hundred years, the common people and the ruling classes didn't understand each other. Some things never change. England now had three language systems. Old English was the everyday language while scholars and the church used Latin. Already, there was a language barrier as the masses who attended church could neither understand nor read the language through which the word of God was transmitted to them.

The Normans added a completely new dimension. The system of government and all legal matters were conducted in French. The common language of the country was English, but within the confines of the castles, the lords and ladies and their staffs - outnumbered 100-1 by the peasants - spoke a Gallic tongue. In order to administer the laws of the land to the commoners, it was necessary to have interpreters. Grammars and dictionaries were needed in order to train the interpreters. Scholars were set to work. However, they were sometimes mistaken when they heard English words. As few of the indigenous population could read or write *englisc* there was a shortage of English men and women who were literate enough to write the words down for the scribes. So, essentially, they often got it wrong! Therefore many English words acquired a French tinge. Likewise, the grammars accelerated the trend to lose the inflections that had been a feature of Old English. A few examples eluded the scribes and are still with us today. Usually we add an *-s* to the end of a word to make the plural. The word *child*, for example, is an exception. This keeps the Old English ending *-en* so that the plural is not *childs* but *children*.

The language was now getting a mixed vocabulary. Old English already had *pig*; the Normans brought *pork*. English had *cow* and *sheep*; French added *beef* and *mutton*. Including Latin, this was a period of trilingual activity that shows up in the language that we speak today. English has at least three words that mean *of or relating to a king or monarch: kingly* from Old English, *royal* from French and *regal* from Latin.

That French did not usurp English is not a mystery. There was no great desire on either side to adopt a new language. Apart from legal matters, the English-speaking peasants had no use for French. If the lords and barons were to spread a new tongue, it would require introducing a very dangerous concept - education. Not wanting to empower the peasants with potentially subversive knowledge, the language gap was a mechanism for social and political control. What did happen though was the Frenchification of English. Even today, some people can't resist dropping a French phrase or *bon mot* into their speech to impress the great unwashed of the general public. A spokesperson for the English National Opera said on Radio 4: "Our *raison* d'être is to perform in English".

By the time of Chaucer this process was well under way. There were new spellings, a huge influx of French and Latin terms and the beginning of the end for the Old English grammar system. Old English became Middle English. The works of Geoffrey Chaucer are important as a record of the language as it was used in the fourteenth century and as a marker point between the changes that had occurred since the Norman invasion and the ones that were yet to come. Chaucer was intricately involved with the upper classes and government, but still found the possibility to use dialect and write bawdy tales. Of course, Chaucer didn't think of Middle English. No-one at the time did because at that time it was modern English, or as there doesn't seem to have been what we would now call linguists, simply English. It only became Middle because in hindsight we can place it in between Old and Modern English. In the future, our successors will undoubtedly revise the term for what we call Modern. By the 14th century the royal court began to increasingly use English. It was partly a result of the fact that the concept of England as a nation was emerging. This was encouraged by the king and the nobility due to the almost constant state of war that existed with France over the former Norman land possessions on the other side of the channel. Recognising English would help the propaganda campaign and the recruitment of troops for campaigns in which they would otherwise have little interest. In 1362, Parliament was opened for the first time with a speech in English. Within the next 50 years, English would more or less replace French in all walks of life.

In 1476, William Caxton set up the first printing press in England. Caxton spotted the idea on a visit to Flanders and realised the commercial possibilities. Caxton had important decisions to make. What kind of language should he use for the books that he intended to print? Spelling and punctuation varied from county to county and even between neighbouring villages as each scribe might have his own individual spelling system. What style of language should he choose; ornate or to appeal to everyone? Inevitably, setting up in London, the local version of what we might call educated English was chosen. Despite putting an unknown number of scribes out of jobs, the printed works that came from Caxton's workshop were still rather inconsistent in terms of language use. But this introduction of printing began a process of standardisation that continues to this day. The process was helped by publications of the bible from John Wycliffe's first translations to the King James Version. Moveable type, the printing of plays and poetry and the novelty of newspapers all continued the trend to standardise English.

Shakespeare did the English language a great service. This can be accepted whether or not you subscribe to the conspiracy theories that the William Shakespeare of Stratford-upon-Avon is not the William Shakespeare of London and that various others such as Marlowe, Jonson, Bacon or the Earl of Oxford wrote one, more or all of Shakespeare's plays. The fact is that Shakespeare provides the best contemporary evidence about the state of English in Elizabethan times. Shakespeare presented many new words, demonstrated the flexibility of English as well as introduced many turns of phrase that are well known to us today. Although Shakespeare used theatrical language that wouldn't necessarily represent how the average person in the street spoke, we can see that Modern English had arrived.

The period from the Renaissance up to the first grammar fascists saw the gradual introduction of modern punctuation. Caxton used only one punctuation mark, the oblique stroke /. Chaucer didn't use any at all.

What was missing now was a dictionary. A schoolmaster called Nathan Bailey had made a good attempt in 1721, but his dictionary definitions were on the casual side, for example, "Horse - beast well-known." Enter Samuel Johnson and his *A Dictionary of the English Language.* Completed in 1755, it had a very important feature. He thought that just saying what a word meant was insufficient as the reader would have to have absolute trust in the compiler. Johnson added illustrative examples (no ipsedixitism here). He also decided that each word should have as many definitions as he could find. One entry describes a zealot as "One passionately ardent in any cause. Generally used in dispraise." Grammar fascists take note. Next to appear are Lowth and Murray.

It could be said that English "just grewed." The language followed no track and went in whatever direction was necessary for communication and pleasure. In modern times, English has become standardised by universal education and acceptance that the language works. But, even so, English is in a state of permanent change, i.e. change that goes on all the time, not change that happens once and is fossilised. Nothing is set in stone and we have to move with the times. Grammar rules are not sacrosanct for evermore. Grammar fascists are conservative by nature. The point of being a pedant is to preserve, not to change or even improve. Therefore despite constant innovation in the language, there are those who can't (or won't) keep up and they certainly are not dedicated followers of fashion. The same is true of vocabulary.

What outraged a grammar fascist yesterday would go unnoticed today. Charles Dickens disliked certain Americanisms such as *reliable* and *healthy*, words that no-one would find unacceptable nowadays. When was the last time you heard someone talk about a colour TV set? This came from the 1960s when black and white TV was the norm and football commentators described the players' shirts in terms of light and dark. Monochrome TVs are the exception nowadays. Can you still buy one? My daughter thinks it odd when I describe my music (or *dadrock* as anything pre-1990 is known) collection as records and talk about LPs. These are areas where different generations have adapted their ways of communication to meet the needs of society. There are kids growing up today who might think that if Romeo and Juliet had text [sic] each other it might have turned out differently.

That isn't to say that we should jump on every language trend. Some are short-lived. Can you remember when *pants* meant *rubbish* or words like *fab, ace, brill, magic, sound, fit, mega* and *gigalicious* were all affirmative words? If you can, then each word dates you. After a lecture on English literature in Stockholm, I asked the speaker if she had moved from England in 1973. She said: "No, 1974. But, you were so close, how did you know?" "Your choice of affirmative words gave it away." As Oscar Wilde pointed out: "Fashion is a form of ugliness so intolerable that we have to alter it every six months." Even so, English is full of energy because it adapts to changing times and ingenious coinings help the language to develop and go forward. So we can thank, or otherwise, the world of fashion for *fashionista, B-list celebrity, must-have, to die for, face of the season, cutting edge, razor-sharp and immaculate.* Progress does not mean abandoning the old. Britain swapped 240 pence for 100 on Monday 14th February 1971. However, decimalisation doesn't seem to have killed the phrase *turn on a sixpence* in motoring columns. The same is true for temperature. On the 11th August 2003, newspapers reported that the temperature reached 100 degrees at Heathrow Airport the day before. That is, degrees Fahrenheit. Come winter, the same papers were reporting temperatures well below zero, freezing point in Celsius. We could resolve this summer/winter dichotomy. When we put the clocks forward in the spring we should move to the Fahrenheit scale and then back to Celsius in the autumn.

Stick-in-the-muds don't want to countenance anything new as they would then have to learn again. So much better to make everyone else meet their ancient standards. Are modern pronunciation, grammar and spelling not too much of a challenge? It is almost as if some people are saying, 'stop the language I want to get off!

I have to wonder if there aren't people who would turn the clock back to more than just imperial units of measurement. I get the impression that there are penists and quillists who somehow belief in the truism that things aren't what they used to be and that there really was a time when English had reached perfection. But when was that time? Should we have stopped the development of English with Chaucer or Shakespeare or Wordsworth or do they mean now? Orwell wrote that every generation imagines itself to be more intelligent than the one that went before it, and wiser than the one that comes after it. Whatever, we have changed. Our lives have changed and our needs for communication have changed, so our language must change. A language that doesn't adapt and change has no vitality. Absence of life, surely, means death, i.e. the end of the line for of the English language.

V What have the Romans ever done for us?

Civilization is a movement and not a condition, a voyage and not a harbor.

Arnold J. Toynbee

Latin was once an extremely useful language to know. For centuries, it was a requirement to be accepted into the world of the learned. It was a language that was politically neutral and was widely used for scholarly papers as they could be read without translation by scholars in other countries. By the 1700s, when English grammar studies were beginning to gain ground, Latin was often used for comparison. Latin is an inflectional language. The function of a word is shown by the ending. The position of the word in a sentence is unimportant. Latin works on morphology, that is, words change their form depending on the meaning. Apart from adding an -s to make a plural, there are very few common word endings in modern English. Because of this, a myth grew up that English had no grammar. This ignored the fact that in English word order is critical to understand the relationship between words. English grammar is based on syntax - the position in the sentence often determines the meaning.

The comparison with Latin was important to the early grammar fascists. They lived in a period of transition. Latin was on the wane and English was spreading to all corners of the world. To say that, of course, is odd. The Earth is a sphere and doesn't have any corners. However, to be accepted by the establishment, you had to know Latin. But that was then and this is now. Latin is a dead language. It has no domain. There is no country that uses the language in daily life. Even in the Vatican City where Latin is prevalent, it isn't the language of communication. Two cardinals in the Sistine Chapel, discussing last night's match between Livorno and Inter Milan, would hardly converse in Latin. Although Ecclesiastical Latin is the official language of the smallest state in the world, it is only used for rituals, ceremonies and documentation. Latin might be pronounced dead but Latin is not extinct. Grammar fascists of today still concern themselves with the strange triviality of trying to hammer the square peg of one language into the round hole of another.

Even before Lowth and his successor, Murray, there was criticism of the Latin influence over English grammar. John Wallis was sent to Oxford to study to become a doctor. He was really interested in mathematics and made a great contribution to the development of algebra, trigonometry and calculus. He was a founding member of the Royal Society and undoubtedly the greatest mathematician of his day. Wallis is credited with inventing the ∞ symbol for infinity. As a graduate, Wallis took the easy option of a career in the priesthood. But he didn't stick at it. Not only was he a puritan, but he got married and had many other things that he wanted to do. As well as becoming an expert on codes and code breaking, he turned his attention to the English language. He wrote a grammar in 1653. In the introduction he clearly cocks a snook at previous attempts to write English grammars.

"They all forced English too rigidly into the mould of Latin, and other things of that kind, giving many useless rules... which have no bearing on our language, and which confuse and obfuscate matters instead of elucidating them."

As a brilliant mathematician he always demanded proof and he wasn't going to let anyone Latinise English without jolly good grounds for it. In his autobiography, Wallis wrote: "It was always my affection, even from a child, not only to learn by rote, but to know the grounds or reasons of what I learnt; to inform my judgement as well as to furnish my memory." No ipsedixitism for John Wallis. Unless someone could show a good reason, Wallis wasn't going to allow the subjugation of English to a foreign tongue. A shame, then, that *Grammatica Linguae Anglicanae* was written in Latin. But apart from wanting membership of the establishment club, Wallis had a very good reason for his choice of language. He saw a great demand from foreigners who wanted to learn English and aimed the book largely at the European market. It was then quite natural to write the grammar in the lingua franca of the age.

Nowadays there are no commercial reasons for using Latin in the study of English. But still grammar fascists persist in their pre-occupation with the language of the Romans.

The most common argument in favour of Latin is that it helps us to understand English, particularly when we look at the plurals of words. For example, what is the plural of *stadium*? The answer, of course, is *stadia*. A travelling show in

Rome might play at one stadium or two stadia. But why should it be so in English? The fact that a word has its origin in Latin doesn't mean that we have to use the Latin plural inflection. English has taken words from just about every major language on the planet without taking the grammar to make the plural. Therefore the answer to the question is, of course, *stadiums*. The spelling checker on my computer rejected the word *stadia*. Instead I was offered *staid*, *studio* and *stadium*. However, unlike grammar fascists who would stop people using *stadiums*, I am more than happy if anyone wishes to use *stadia* as the plural as long as everyone else can understand. The vast majority of the world's one billion plus users of English have absolutely no knowledge of the deceased language in question and would struggle to make *stadia* from *stadium*. In dictionaries both plurals are listed. I cannot resist pointing out that in every one of the ten dictionaries that I looked at *stadiums* was listed first. Ha! In any case, the Latin lovers are on dodgy ground with *stadia* as it is Greek in origin coming from *stadion*. I wonder if that means we have to consider Greek plural endings as well. Why don't we hold a referendum on the question? But first we should hold a referendum on the purpose of a referendum. Which means we will need two referendums (or should it be two referenda?). In Latin *referendum* means 'thing to be referred' or, in other words, 'the question to be decided.' Nowadays, however, the English word is understood by most people to mean 'a vote on the question to be decided.' So we need a referendum in the ancient meaning to decide what the question is and then a referendum in the modern sense to answer the question.

Data is plural but is treated as if it were singular. I can't imagine anyone saying that 'the data are good.' The singular is *datum*, but this word is rarely heard. *Agenda* is similar. *Agendum* was the original singular, but now we have one *agenda* or separate *agendas*. Q*uorum* only has an English plural, i.e. *quorums*. *Media* is a word that causes grammar fascists to suck in air each time it is used in phrases such as: 'through the media of television.' In common usage people do not generally refer back to whether the original Latin was plural or singular. The driving factor in all these cases is communication not adherence to questionable grammar rules.

Confusion about the latinisation of plurals results in hypercorrection. If we apply the principle of *reductio ad absurdum* (reduction to the absurd), we could think that the plural of bus is not buses. It should be *bi*. The supposition is that Latin words with the singular ending in *-us,* take *-i* in the plural (syllabus-syllabi and gladiolus-gladioli, etc). As an abbreviated form of *omnibus,* meaning 'for all,' bus is of Latin origin, so the plural is indeed *bi*. This shows the nonsense of applying the rules of Latin to English, especially so as in this case the general interpretation of the rule is not entirely correct. We would need to know whether omnibus belongs to the second declension. So we would have to learn a significant amount of Latin to be able to correctly identify English plurals. Without this knowledge the plurals of English words of Latin or Greek origin are unpredictable. Also, you have to know which words originate in which language. A supposition exists that the plural of hippopotamus is *hippopotami*. But the word is of Greek origin and shouldn't therefore have a Latin plural. However, so many people say hippopotami that most dictionaries list it as an alternative to *hippotamuses*.

Why burden people with unnecessary complication in English? This is an issue that really concerns what is more pleasant to the speaker. That is, unless your purpose with saying *syllabi* instead of *syllabus* is simply the hope that people will think that you are cleverer than you really are. *Omnia dicta fortiora si dicta Latina* translates roughly as 'everything sounds more impressive when said in Latin.'

I regularly receive letters calling me Latin names. However, when contacted by alumni relations of either of the two universities that I attended, I avoid being an alumnus by calling myself a *former student*. These two academic institutions are only interested in alumni as they think we might care to donate money to our old *alma mater* (another term I won't thank the Romans for) if we think that the university still cares about us and what we are up to. *Alma mater* is Latin for *nourishing mother*. Well, I got little maternal care during my formal learning and I blame my letter-day fondness for cold baked beans straight from the tin upon periods of under-nourishment that they nowadays call being an undergraduate. The term is derived from the motto *Alma Mater Studiorum*. This comes from what is generally thought to be the oldest European university, the University of Bologna. It seems to have been forgotten that the two ancient and noble educational establishments that I attended predate Bologna by millennia. These are The School of Hard Knocks and The University of Life.

Early *LatinaNazis* caused unnecessary complication in the English spelling system by adding silent letters. The weird spellings of words like *debt* and *doubt* were created during the 1500s. The blame rests squarely on the shoulders of scholars suffering from a kind of false memory syndrome. The two words above reached English via the French *dette* and *doute*. The silent *b* was added to make the words more like the Latin *debitum* and *dubitare*. Maybe these busybodies wanted to give us some kind of history lesson in order to teach us the origins of the French words in the language of the Romans. They also added the quite unnecessary and useless *g* to *reign*. An even worse crime against English was to suppose that the Latin *insula* was the origin of *island*. Perhaps they thought that Latin was a superior language and therefore it was much better to have a word originate from the cultured Romans than from the barbaric Anglo-Saxons. In addition and incorrectly, they put the silent *s* into *island*. The Romans were civilised, the scholars who misinterpreted English can only be regarded as Vandals. Sadly, Latinanazis are still at work today.

There are some grammar fascists who advocate teaching Latin in schools. There is some weird idea that translating from one language to the other teaches English grammar because the languages are so similar. We have already seen that Latin is inflectional and English is syntactic. So much for similarity. There are a number of quotations on the subject that are as boring as they are long and therefore have no place here. But reading between the lines I get rather mixed signals: It is almost as if the message is that the lack of literacy that some people perceive in modern society is not due to poverty, social injustice, absence of parental support, teaching methods or anything else. It's all down to ignorance of a dead language. Even the assertion that by knowing Latin one can be more precise in English is false. There are hundreds of millions of English speakers around the world who communicate in a perfectly acceptable and accurate way without ever having learnt a word of Latin. The justification often used for allowing the influence of Latin is the number of English words that have Latin origins. English is usually thought of as a Germanic language, yet only a quarter of the vocabulary is of Old English (Anglo-Saxon), Viking, Dutch or German origin. Around 28% of all English words have Latin origins. Almost the same percentage comes from French, most of these originating from Latin. But we don't need to know Latin to be able to recognise the meanings of words. Most of these are fully integrated into English, so they aren't Latin words anymore. Even when Latin terms are used directly they may be understood. Most readers could work out an approximate meaning of *reductio ad absurdum* above without looking at a translation. Michael Beresford in *Modern English* wrote about a Latin fallacy. He noted that "Latin tradition dominated and distorted the teaching of English." He continued: "Only when the science of linguistics came to the fore in the late 19th century was it generally realised that English could not be satisfactorily described or explained in terms of the rules governing Latin."

Latin is useful, though. I studied the subject for two years at school. Thanks to Latin I can read old gravestones in cathedrals and I have indelibly stamped upon my mind such indispensable phrases as *agricolae fugare bant*[1]. I can go to Italy and recognise a remarkable amount of Italian. Latin has also helped me with French and Spanish. It has given me an insight into the structure of language that was extremely useful when I studied Faroese, the language of the Faroe Islands. However, as a role model for English, Latin is about as much use as sun-tan lotion on a wet weekend in Weymouth.

The bloody Romans (as opposed to the peaceful ones) have given us a linguistic legacy that does have one domain, the garden. The two-word system of naming plants invented by Carl von Linné is a very reasonable use of Latin. It avoids provoking national sensitivities that might arise when a newly discovered plant is given a name that is offensive in another language. It does not allow different plants to have a name in common. A Swedish bluebell is quite unlike the British plant with the same name. The system is also useful when a plant has different names according to location. What is commonly known as cow parsley in England is called by a number of names in

---

[1]Meaning: 'The farmers were put to flight' - a phrase I use constantly.

Sweden including *dog biscuit*. The botanical name is the same in all countries, *Anthriscus sylvestris*.

So, what did the Romans do for us? A general perception is that the Romans were the good guys, especially compared to all those nasty Goths. They brought us baths, central heating and, well, law and order. After all, Latin in English is a lot of hocus pocus. The common belief is that *hocus pocus* is a corruption of the Latin words used during communion: *Hoc est (enim) corpus (meum),* 'this is my body'. Most of the congregation, not being able to understand Latin, took the words to symbolise something that was incomprehensible. Therefore hocus pocus came to mean nonsense, trickery or deception, especially so, as the words accompanied the mystery turning wine into blood and bread into flesh. Most likely, hocus pocus first appeared in the 1600s as an incantation used by magicians, conjurors and sleight of hand artists although there isn't sufficient evidence available. What we do know is that hocus pocus, whether Latin or not, is most probably the source of another common English word: *hoax*. The word is quite adequate to describe the false amalgamation of English into Latin. Anyway, it's all Greek to me.

6. Whose language is it anyway?

Property is theft

Pierre-Joseph Proudhon

Who owns English? The answer is every one and no-one. However, certain people think that they call the tune in the language. And, sadly, most people seem to have given their tacit acceptance to having our language controlled. Sorry? Our language is being controlled by someone? No, surely not. This is the stuff of fiction. Think so? Well let's have at look a work of fiction and compare with reality. George Orwell wrote the novel *Nineteen Eighty-Four* as an example of dystopia, in this case, an example of how society could degenerate if we allow power to become concentrated in a few hands. The book was set in a future where a totalitarian regime has assumed power. English has been replaced by a synthetic language called *Newspeak*. The new language is based on English (now called *Oldspeak*). The purpose of the language is to make any alternative thinking impossible by removing words or constructions that oppose the dictatorial regime. The concept of freedom, for example, would be eliminated over time. Orwell invented the concept of *Thought Police* who would enforce the compliance of the vast majority of the population.

The year 1984 has long passed and there is still no authority that controls the English language. Other countries have organisations with more or less prescriptive roles. The Swedish Academy has designated the Swedish noun for electronic messages to be e-post and the verb e-posta. This is quite logical as Sweden has a postal system and this is electronic post. In English speaking countries, e-mail has been generally adopted, an Americanisation that reflects the fact that in the USA they use mail as a noun and verb rather than post in Britain, Australia and so on. The US dominates computer language. The Swedes are split between the home-baked e-post and the more international sounding e-mejl which is pronounced pretty much as in English. The Swedish Academy's dictionary is not binding and people are free to choose. The French have a renowned academy that is the official authority on the usage of their language. However, the French Academy can only recommend. In the late 1970s, they wanted to stem the tide of Anglicisation and proscribe certain English loan word constructions such as le week-end and un parking. I recently spent un weekend in Perpignan and had no trouble booking a hotel using that term for Friday to Sunday or finding the place where to put the car. Franglais seems to be alive and well. The French have even made up English words that no Brit or Yank would recognise. There is a term un relooking, meaning a makeover. There is even an L'Institut De Relooking International in Paris that teaches personal image and style. Regarding the internet, the governments in Paris and Quebec have proposed using the French term courrier électronique. The French use e-mail and mail just like everyone else as well as the homespun mèl. Courrier electronique is too long and is only really used by French grammar fascists and in formal e-mails. Even then it is shortened to courriel. Essentially then, when free to do so, they have taken little notice of the 'immortals' of the French Academy. They are free spirits and don't want anyone telling them what to do.

Orwell's fears for society did not materialise and the attempts of countries to persuade and recommend their citizens to use language in a certain way have come to nothing[1].

So the bold statement that I made at the beginning cannot be true. However, English is manipulated and controlled and some seek more influence over the language. Allow me to explain. By allowing the grammar fascists the opportunity to occupy the moral high ground, we have given them free reign over the language, in effect, granted them ownership. Every time an apostropharian derides a greengrocer for writing POTATO'S on a sign, or a self-appointed language police corrects a double negative, we see an attempt to control English. More subtle than taking the official route, but the effect is the same. By adopting a superior tone and attempting to induce uncertainty and doubt in others, the grammar fascists insidiously enforce their rules. Orwell invented another term. In his own words: "There is a word in Newspeak, I don't know whether you know it: *duckspeak*, to quack like a duck. It is one of those interesting words that have two contradictory meanings. Applied to an opponent, it is abuse; applied to someone you agree with, it is praise." Duckpeak is a major tool for grammar fascists. They scorn what they see as bad English,

---

[1]Icelandic and Faroese are two languages that have not succumbed to the imperialism of English.

but would condone any abuse of English that suits their purpose. Poor language often comes with labels such as sloppiness, anarchy, lack of morals, bad education, etc. But who made those associations and put those labels there? The grammar fascists label contemporary English usage as 'decline' in order to justify imposing rules.

Did you know that there is an organisation called the Queen's English Society "dedicated to preserving the beauty and precision of the English language." Recently the QES sent a 5,000 word submission to the BBC. I haven't read it and I have no inclination to. However, I know that a prominent member of the QES complains that while the BBC has a pronunciation unit, the Corporation has no body dealing with vocabulary or grammar. This particular grammar fascist (I am sure that the organisation itself has truly noble aims) has held a long-term grudge against the BBC. He even blames television coverage of Wimbledon (and Jimmy Connors) for the grunting noise that tennis players make when they serve. This man, Ian Bruton-Simmonds, says: "...the BBC is the most influential broadcaster in the English-speaking world! And its indifference to Standard English prevails in broadcasting throughout the English-speaking world and it therefore prevails in the schools." Apart from the absurdity of his argument and the fact that Mr Bruton-Simmonds seems unable to express himself without repeating the same phrase twice, he is trying to pull the wool over everyone's eyes. His claims are based purely on what he regards as acceptable. Grammar fascists possibly see themselves as linguistic guardians, but people like this want to restrict the use of English to only the kind of which they approve. We should be thankful to George Orwell for giving us the word *duckspeak*.

The aim of pressure groups such as the QES is to encourage standard English. But exactly where is standard English to be found? The Queen's English is the obvious answer. But how many people talk like the Queen? The lady in Buckingham Palace speaks a kind of English called RP, *Received Pronunciation* - a dialect of English, that some people might simply call talking posh. But less than 3% of the population speak RP. Surely the grammar fascists wouldn't want us all to standardise our speech based on such a small base of users? Also, the age of deference has passed. The style of the monarch is not a role model for the masses, if it ever was. We now live in an age of reason, a meritocracy, where one's vowel sounds, rounded or otherwise should not be a barrier to success. I fear that the Queen's English Society are living the past.

Oh, and just a quick question for the grammar fascists. If we are talking about the Queen's English shouldn't we have to get permission to use her language? The apostrophe in *Queen's* surely denotes that it indeed belongs to Her Majesty.

Another term substituted for standard English is *Oxford English*. Oxford in this case means the university and not the city; the 'dreaming spires' as opposed to the production line of the BMW plant at Cowley. There is no standard in Oxford, indeed anyone visiting the city might wonder about the language, such are the numbers of tourists and parties of students uttering anything but English. The *Oxford English Dictionary* represents a standard of some kind, but the role of this great enterprise, apart from being restricted to one area of language, vocabulary, is to report the language as it is used, not to set a benchmark for comparison.

BBC English is another term that is bandied about in the hunt for a role model. However, the language used by the BBC is varied and diverse. There are 40 local radio stations in England alone. Each of these reflects regional and even parochial patterns of speech. BBC English has changed; no longer do the educated elite read the news in Received Pronunciation dressed in dinner jackets at Alexandra Palace studios. The BBC is an inclusive organisation that reflects the modern society we live in. As we have seen, some grammar fascists contend that the BBC is no longer an institution to be admired and copied because it has furthered the decline in language by letting oiks from the sticks sit in front of microphones and present TV shows.

The level of debate about standards has been set by the grammar fascists themselves. They have posed the question as which standard should be applied to English. The discussion should be about the possibility of finding a standard. Only then can we look for one. In the meantime, we should concentrate on finding the norms of English in current usage. However, the problem is that there are so many irregularities. If grammars differ in their prescriptions depending on where, when and by whom they were written, then usage varies even more widely.

The following chapters take a rummage around the English language to examine some its inconsistencies and idiosyncrasies.

7. Grammar school

You Are What You Is.

Frank Zappa

This chapter takes issue with just a few of the flawed grammar rules that Lowth and Murray, along with their modern counterparts, would inflict onto the language. I hope to show that self-fulfilling prophecies and after constructions do not justify restricting the use of the language.

Perhaps there is one element of English that, above all others, will cause a state of apoplexy. This is the issue that still upsets the average British grammar fascist, the split infinitive. Did you notice the use of *to harshly judge* in chapter one? Did you care? If so, your Grammar (fascist) Index (GI) is rising and maybe it's time for the GI diet. Possibly the most infamous split infinitive is amongst the opening lines of the science fiction series *Star Trek*: "The mission: ...to boldly go where no man has gone before." When first broadcast on NBC in the USA in 1966, I guess that this sentence did not so much as raise an eyebrow. However, when the series was shown on this side of the Atlantic, the collective indignation of the nation was aired in typical British fashion, a flood of letters to the newspapers and the BBC.

The split infinitive issue is vehemently disputed, although I would vehemently dispute that it is such a controversial subject. Why is it that I can write 'I would vehemently dispute' but not 'to vehemently dispute?' Vehemently is an adverb. In both cases vehemently describes the degree of dispute. This is just another example of the inconsistency of the pedants' arguments. But, there is no compelling reason to put the adverb before or after the verb that it describes. Surely it is again a matter of taste. You either like it or you don't.

There are times when the position of the adverb does matter. Imagine a teacher at the end of a lesson saying: "I really want you to pack up quickly" or "I want you to pack up really quickly" or "I want you to really pack up quickly." I could imagine all three possibilities, each with a slightly different meaning. In the first, *really* describes the teacher's wish. In the second, it describes how fast the packing up should be done. But then there is the third meaning. *Really* changes the nature of the sentence. Here it is not a request, but comes over more as a command. The grammar fascists would deny use of the third option as the infinitive is split. So what they are doing, apart from following an imagined rule, is putting a stop to a wonderful piece of flexibility in English. They would therefore not allow teachers one of the most important tools in their arsenal of verbal weapons, i.e. to make an instruction sound like a request.

Four decades after *Star Trek*, the BBC are now doing it for themselves. In one of the property programmes that now seem to be ubiquitous on the daytime TV schedules, a BBC presenter invited the prospective purchaser of a house "to properly investigate." This is BBC English, no problem surely? Or, some people might maintain this is the problem with the BBC.

There have been some famous infinitive splitters including Wordsworth, Coleridge, Byron,

Henry James and Thomas Hardy. George Bernard Shaw was typically outspoken on the subject. Shaw once wrote to his publisher after a proof-reader had corrected a split infinitive: "I call for the immediate dismissal of this pedant...It is of no concern to me whether he decides to go quickly or to quickly go."

One of the greatest experts on the English language was Danish, Otto Jespersen. He said that the split infinitive was, in any case, a fiction. He pointed out that *to* does not belong to the infinitive any more than *the* goes with a noun. If we can't allow *to boldly go*, we can't accept *the big tree* as the adjective splits the noun.

The split infinitive is a lurking, modern-day shibboleth. It distinguishes those who know and cherish out-dated language from those who neither know, nor care. Whether the latter group are uninterested or disinterested is not relevant. The only function of being able to identify this language construction is to add some meaning to the otherwise sad lives of people with nothing better to do. My concluding advice to the grammar fascists on this issue is to immediately cease, to once and for all give up and to never again criticise the split infinitive.

Supermarkets provide much material for anyone interested in language. In fact, almost every supermarket in the English-speaking world has a sword of Damocles hanging quite literally over the customers' heads. The next time that you are in a supermarket and intend to checkout with such standards of British cuisine as sushi rice, tikka masala sauce and nothing else, proceed to the queue where trolleys are not allowed and look up.

The chances are that a sign will display a message such as "5 items or less." The time-poor executive manager will be grumbling under his breath that the person in front has 6 items. That person then turns round and mouths "BOGOF." Not an insult, but an explanation: "Buy One Get One Free". Therefore the free item doesn't break the rule. For the pedant, however, this opens up a whole new basket of tinned tuna. The grammar fascists will be tut-tut-tutting at the transgression of a much more hallowed and traditional "rule" (and remember traditional nowadays means anything that you have done more than once, e.g. trick or treating at Halloween has become a tradition in the last 2 years). The 11th commandment in the Grammar fascist's bible does not govern how many items but the choice of words. *Fewer* is used with countables, i.e. more than one of something where the plural ends in *s,* for example 'there are fewer apples in the bargain pack than last week.' *Less* is used where the amount is uncountable or is a degree of measurement, for example 'there is less than a kilo of apples in the bargain pack this week.'[1] So 5 items or less should be 5 items or fewer! Miss Jones would be oh-so proud of me! The monolithic plot by the supermarket cartels to deface the language has been exposed. No. What we should accept is that *X items or less* has become an idiomatic phrase. The grammar fascists are pushing against an open door. Professor Svartvik of Lund University said 25 years ago that this was common in informal English,

---

[1] I use this guideline: less means not as much while fewer means not as many.

even if it wasn't generally accepted. The fact is that supermarket signs have become accepted by general usage. There are exceptions to the supposed rule anyway. What about these to do with distance, amount or time: less than 500 miles, less than £50, less than 5 months. There is also the expression *no less than*, as in no less than 10 shoppers joined in the brawl that marred the opening of a mall. If you disagree with this, please send me an e-mail stating your reasons in 20 words or less. Once again, this rule is relatively recent. Using less with countables has only been frowned upon since the 1700s. It is all a matter of idiom rather than poor communication. We might hear someone say: "There are less than a dozen bargain packs of apples left, should I buy them all, dear?" We might think, hmm, that's not quite right, is it? But we all understand the message: "They are almost sold out, grab one quick."

Before we leave the shop it's time to chew over that old chestnut whether it is OK to end a sentence with a preposition. That is, apart from the other old chestnut whether good writing should include abbreviations of dubious origin such as *OK*, is another Lowth-Murray axis-of-evil-grammar piece of nonsense. People should be allowed to make up their own minds. If you don't like it don't do it. But there are folks who aren't bothered, so don't bother them. The question is not *why*, but *why not?* To those who might demand that a sentence does not end with a preposition, I would simply like to pose my own question: "What is the world coming to? After all, a preposition is a good thing to end a sentence with."

'Now,' as the voice-over between TV programmes tells us 'is the moment that you have all been waiting for.' Well, when I say all, I mean those of you who know that I have long debated this aspect of language. Actually it isn't that many compared to the hoped-for readership of this book. So, not all, but some. And in all truth, just a few.

It is time to take issue with the Lindley Murray myth about the double negative. Inspector Morse, the detective of novel and television, was somewhat of a grammar fascist and crossword solver. I say *was* because Morse was killed off by his creator, Colin Dexter. I know this because when I was in Oxford, I visited the location where tourists take pictures of the spot where Morse had his fatal heart attack and where fiction blurs with fact. "Surely it was little to the left?" "But if the camera was placed in the third window up there, he would have to have died just here." "Right, come on everyone, otherwise we won't get to Tolkien's house by three o'clock" breaks the discussion about the exact point of Morse's death. But we, like the tourists, will suspend our disbelief for a moment. When Morse was alive and castigating his sergeant for his use of the split infinitive, he may have come across a suspect who said: "I ain't done nothing, Morse." To which Oxford's most famous police inspector replies: "I ain't done nothing. What kind of language is that? Two negatives make a positive. Therefore, he has done something. Lewis, charge him. This man is guilty!"

This is the famous double negative fallacy. It is based upon mathematical logic. In mathematics when adding two figures together that both have a minus value, the result will be a positive number.

In the example of Morse and his suspect, *ain't* and *nothing* cancel each other out. As a mathematical concept, it works like this:

ain't	nothing
-1	-1

$(-1) + (-1) = 1$ In other words a positive.

So in London where there is a pandemic of double negatives, it means instant guilt. But the real criminals are Murray and the followers who concocted the equation. Why apply maths to language? The answer is simply to invent a pseudo-scientific explanation for something that the founding fathers of grammar fascism of didn't like. If only the anti-double negative brigade were to come clean. If they admitted that they find this way of speaking inelegant or hard on the ear, then I would have some understanding for their viewpoint. At least it would be an honest opinion, but still only an opinion. For it is quite possible that the aim of a double, triple or greater negative is to add emphasis. This is an example of African-American vernacular speech.

"No way no girl can't wear no platform shoes to no amusement park"

This is the sequence and mathematical equation for that sentence.

No	no	can't	no	no
-1	-1	-1	-1	-1

(-1) + (-1) + (-1) + (-1) + (-1) = -1 A negative!

In this case the speaker is quite justified as the number of negatives is an odd number. Two pairs of negatives cancel each other out leaving one negative. The girl can't wear the platform shoes. The mathematical argument falls when there is 3, 5, 7 or any odd number of negatives.

Grammar, though, is not maths; the speaker is adding negatives for emphasis. What he really means is ABSOLUTELY NOT!

On the television quiz show, *Have I Got News For* You? Boris Johnson MP said: "I could not fail to disagree with you less." Who is more clear, the African-American speaker of the Member of Parliament for Henley? For his comment, Mr Johnson was given the 2004 The Foot in Mouth award by the Plain English Campaign

Here is a double negative that aroused some controversy:

> We don't need no education.
> We don't need no thought control.

This comes from the song *Another brick in the wall* by Pink Floyd. Popular music is peppered with double negatives. The Rolling Stones belted out *I can't get no satisfaction* and Elvis Presley joyfully sang *You ain't nothing but a hound dog.* Johnny Cash recorded a Bert Williams song. The chorus is:

Well, I ain't never done nothing to nobody.
I ain't never got nothing from nobody, no time.
And, until I get something from somebody sometime,
I don't intend to do nothing for nobody, no time.

Is there anyone who would care to apply the mathematical grammar 'logic' to those four lines? Multiple negatives can be entertaining. One of the purposes of language can be pure pleasure.
The world of TV would be all the poorer too if American cops weren't allowed to burst in on a gang of gangsters and shout "Don't nobody move."

Double negatives were a feature of both Old and Middle English. Chaucer, for example, was no stranger to them. The present bias against double negatives was introduced in the 1700s, supposedly as a way of making English logical. Most people fell for it and continue to do so today.

Some people claim that there are acceptable double negatives. I don't disagree, even if the use is one of those exceptions that prove a rule. For this is the catch-all cry that allows grammar fascists to be inconsistent while seeming to uphold the rule of law in English and, importantly, not losing face. *I don't disagree* is a variation of double negation. But while this construction meets muster, the *I ain't done nothing* type of double negative is unacceptable. Is it the mathematical equation at work? No, the negative elements *don't* and *dis* do not cancel each other out. *I don't disagree* is not the same as *I agree.* The difference is a question of degree, lying somewhere between opposition and concurrence. The double negative increases the flexibility of the language. Does that reason alone justify this kind of double negative or is it a question of personal preference? Does one kind of multiple negative sound learned and the other unsophisticated? The grammar fascist was not incompetent, simply judgemental.

If using double negatives does lead to misunderstanding, surely there can only be one approach. Rather than criticise, simply ask for clarification. To those who use multiple negatives, beware of the grammar fascists lying in ambush. Simplify your expression so as not to confuse these simple people who are unable or unwilling to make sense of what you have to say.

As long as I can remember there has been a debate about when to use *who* or *whom*. I am not even going to start on that discussion. Most people have been touched in some way by this 'rule' (you are supposed to use *whom* after a preposition, right?). It is not unusual to correct someone or be corrected while misusing *whom* (so, if it isn't linked to a preposition, when do I use it?). Most of the correcting is done by people who want others to know of their superiority. With all the assertiveness of a Lowth or a Murray, they fool the rest of us by displaying 100% confidence that they are right. So, even though we suspect they aren't completely accurate as the 'rule' is actually not that simple, our own doubts restrain us from entering into a discussion. At the end of the last century, the letters page of the *Sunday Telegraph* had the headline: "Morse falls victim to poor grammar" and discussed the use of *whom*. Because of letters like this, most people play safe and just don't use *whom* at all. Apart from in the phrase, *to whom it may concern*, *whom* is disappearing and perhaps runs the risk of extinction. This is sad. I actually think that we should use *whom*. Not for the reason that it can make us sound more refined, rather simply for the sake of diversity. If you have gathered anything thus far from this book, you will understand that a dislike of uniformity is one of my prime concerns. If we replace *whom* with *who* all the time, we lose a word in the language, we lose an alternative way of expression and another discussion point for those interested in language.

Question: What kind of language uses adjectives like English? Answer: English. Although English can be a noun as well as an adjective, such are the opportunities that we have the language. The comparative and superlative of *good* are *better* and *best*. For *bad* they are, respectively, *worse* and *worst*. Not the most logical perhaps, but again a result of the mixed history of the language. Under the heading "A common error?" a correspondent to a national newspaper complained about the use of *commoner*. He cited this phrase as an example "…is four times commoner in boys." He went on to point out that commoner means a person not belonging to the nobility. The correspondent is dismissing the inflectional form (shown by the ending) and indicating a preference for the phrasal form (adding more or most). *Common, commoner, commonest* or *common, more common, most common*. I have a personal preference as, no doubt, will all readers.

However, whose place is it to say that someone who chooses differently is incorrect.

The language allows us to use both forms in many cases. I tried to make up a rule for myself to show when an adjective should take one form or another. I examined all kinds of factors including the number of syllables and whether or not the adjective ended with a certain letter or combination of letters. I failed. I was unable to come up with even a guideline. So it should remain a preference. I was asked by a Swedish teacher how I decided which was the most acceptable. My reply was simply to say both the inflectional and phrasal forms out loud. If one sounds awkward, difficult to pronounce or just plain ridiculous, then surely only the alternative form would do. She asked me what was the most acceptable. By saying most acceptable out loud and comparing with acceptablest, I was able to prove my point. To rub the point home, I also said "bad, worser, worsest". However, the odd thing is that bestest does exist. In the USA a child might announce someone as "my bestest friend". This arises because everyone has to be a best friend, so that no-one is placed in the lower class of being just a friend. In making a long-winded but hopefully complete justification of my answer, I went a step further by trying another:

Inflectional	Phrasal
happy	happy
happier	more happy
happiest	most happy

I then made up a sentence comparing each form of a comparable adjective. In this case, they both work. So once again we come down to a matter of choice; what is more pleasant to the ear or least offensive to the eye? Then we come to another issue, that of double marked adjectives, for example: English is more easier than French and mistakes are most commonest in spoken English. I have no statistical evidence, but I am sure that this double marking is becoming more common, especially in speech. Indeed, I would go as far as to say it is more common than when I was a child myself interacting with other children and we all spoke to each other using some kind of drivel-driven grammar. Exactly the same as when grown-ups today use expressions such as most perfect and quite unique. I suggest that rather than ignorance of grammar, this is just part of the hyperbole that pervades our language these days. People are simply trying to express themselves forcefully to indicate the extent to which they feel about a subject.

A bugbear of grammar fascists is a sentence beginning with *and*. *And* is a conjunction for joining two parts of a sentence, therefore it can't be at the beginning of a sentence. Chaucer did it. It is fine with one of the holy scriptures that grammar fascists use to beat miscreants with, Fowler's *Modern English Usage.* William Blake didn't mind it. Britain's favourite poem, set to music as a hymn, sung by the Women's Institute, rugby crowds, conservatives and socialists alike begins: "And did those feet..." One of the oldest surviving texts written in Britain, the Venerable Bede's

Ecclesiastical History of the English People, begins with "Et Britannia insula est." And Britain is an island.[1] No comfort for the Latin revivalists there.

For the church-going, I issue an invitation to open the King James Bible. After the opening verse, 29 of the next 30 verses all begin with *and*.

There never has been a rule to forbid *and* at the beginning of a sentence, but generations of school teachers simply regarded it as inelegant.

Verbing is a self-explanatory name for a wonderful process where words change their class. It's a bit like when a council house kid becomes a teacher. The root remains the same, but working class becomes middle. When it comes to words, the process is about nouns becoming verbs. Verbing is not a widely known term in the United Kingdom, but the process of verbing has been experienced by most people. And, it is bound to raise the hackles of many a grammar fascist. The best way to illustrate the concept is to give some examples. A recent newspaper headline announced: "Nobel Prize for revolutionising medicine." An American company, known for the shops where you can make photocopies used the advertising slogan: "Kinkos - the better place to office." Stuck at an airport after my flight was cancelled, I was told: "The later flight today is fully booked, but I can waitlist you it."

---

[1]*Et* can also mean *also* e.g. during the murder of Julius Caesar. "Et tu, Brute." Why should he begin by pointing out that Britain is also an island, as he hadn't written anything previously? Bede's history could be the source of the incorrect origin of *island* that was mentioned in the previous chapter.

The concept may well be disliked because each verbing[1] generates a new word. Grammar fascists, as we have seen, are arch-conservatives when it comes to the English language. However, without verbing we would be stuck with a more limited language. I was once *admitted to hospital* to get my badly broken nose fixed. Ten years later, I was *hospitalised* after a road traffic accident. The different use of language was irrelevant. On each occasion, I discovered just how great the National Health Service is. When the ambulance is coming, you don't complain about verbing! *Verbification* (I think I will stick with verbing) may be derided as slang. But the headline that I cited is from a broadsheet and was selected from a very long list that I have collected. Perhaps the biggest objection is that many verbs should never have been made when there is already a perfectly good way of saying the same thing.

Why *prioritise* something when we can *make something a priority*? Consider this newspaper statement: "Green was tasked by Margaret Thatcher to deport the dissident." The other option is to have written: 'Green was given the task of deporting the dissident by Margaret Thatcher.' The former is more succinct. It can make a pretentious expression much shorter and more concise. Look at this sentence: "The Hutton inquiry

[1]To delight any errant quillist who might just be reading by candlelight, I applied a computer spellchecker to verbing. I was offered four corrections, verging, veering, kerbing and herbing. I *conject* that grammar fascists might regard verbing as veering away from the language and that it should be kerbed (sic)!

will accuse the Government this week of forcing the civil service to politicise its use of intelligence on Iraq." Try to replace *politicise* with any less than four other words and, importantly, retain the original meaning. Hopefully, you will see that verbing really is useful.

Verbing has always been a feature of English. Shakespeare certainly did his share of verbing. It is a natural process of development in language. In historical terms, this is a chicken and egg situation. Which came first the noun or the verb? It doesn't matter. The point is that we can make nouns into verbs and vice versa. We can send a text and we can text someone. Having both the noun and the verb allows flexibility. Why should anyone care which construction is used? *To chair a meeting* is a rather useful expression and describes exactly the function of the chair(person). Many business, political and social meetings would be more awkward without the possibility *to chair*.

There is a great deal of inconsistency in complaints about verbing. Take the verb to exit. "Wayne Rooney exits Everton" was a headline that I read on an internet website. A critique soon appeared on the website's message board to the effect that, 'one makes an exit, but does not exit.' But I wonder if the theatrical direction to 'Exit stage left' would raise the same objection.

I defend verbing, even when it sounds odd for, after all, verbing only sounds odd when it is new. In time the novelty wears off. But there is a tendency to over-do some verbed words. The use of *impact* replacing *affect* is one that comes to mind as in this is recent quotation from a broadsheet: "Technology impacted on the popularity of the guitar..." My objection concerns lack of imagination in choosing a varied vocabulary.

Can any word be verbed? I found an article by a grammar fascist complaining about *fooding* as an example of verbing when there is the perfectly adequate *feeding*. I did some elementary research and found that *fooding* was invented by Alexandre Cammas as a concept to emphasise a style choice, combining the type of cuisine to factors such as where and how food is taken. Fooding is a French word following the trend set by the many Franglais terms that take an English word and add *-ing*. So the whole premise for criticising the word was false. As we know, that is all too often the pedant's way. I once knew a chap called Max Matthews who was an excellent office equipment salesman. He had a little saying: "All buyers are liars." What he meant was that usually a potential customer doesn't give the true reason for not making a purchase. 'I don't like the colour' might be stated instead of 'it's too expensive.' A good salesman has a shed load of reasons to justify a high price, but not very much to say if the only colour available is battleship grey. So it is with the grammar fascists. They are dishonest to the core. The real reasons might be: I don't like it, it's inelegant, it sounds American, etc. Instead, they will invent a pseudo- grammatical explanation. Why the obfuscation? Is it really so difficult to admit that judgements and priorities are often a matters of taste?

8. My word!

In two words, im possible.

Samuel Goldwyn

There are some issues pertaining to vocabulary that make grammar fascists feel uncomfortable; one is that words change over time. *Gay* is a good example. Any teacher of English will tell you that finding this word in works by Jane Austen or the Brontë sisters is guaranteed to elicit a collective snigger from a class; most recently for more than one reason. An early meaning from the Old French *gai* was 'having or showing a joyous mood' or 'bright or showy.' From the late 17th century *gay* also had the sexual connotation of 'uninhibited by moral constraints.' During the Victorian period, 'gay life' became a well-established euphemism for prostitution and other forms of extramarital sexual behaviour that were perceived as immoral. Somewhere between Oscar Wilde and Noël Coward the meaning referring to prostitution disappeared and gay also came to mean homosexual. Coward used gay in this context in a song called "Green Carnation." It alluded to Oscar Wilde, who famously wore such a flower. The homosexual meaning was at first a sort of code as homosexuality was illegal. The homosexual and theatrical communities in London had their own open-secret language called *Polari*. Gay became used more openly in the 1950s and from the 1970s has been truly out of the linguistic closet. Sometime during the nineties it even became gender specific as the term lesbian and gay gained ground and differentiated male and female homosexuals. Then, sometime around the turn of the last century, gay acquired yet another sense. In school playgrounds, children began to use it as meaning *naff* or *useless*. The BBC dealt with a complainant who argued that the use of gay in this context was homophobic. The committee said that this was an additional meaning and simply kept up with developments in English usage as it was often now used to mean 'lame' or 'rubbish.' Gay, therefore, has undergone a transition from meaning bright to something rather dull.

My mother was once an *air hostess* with BOAC. When men came to do the same work as well, the job title changed to *air steward* or *stewardess*. Nowadays, *flight attendant* is the usual term. Words change their meanings through time. Remember *decimate*? There is little that anyone can do if enough people accept an additional or changed meaning of a word. Some grammar fascists are victims of etymological fallacy. This is a misconception based on the idea that the etymology (history or origin) of a word or phrase is the actual meaning. It also supposes that the etymology is correct in the first place.

There is a kind of grammar fascist who is almost benign and finds the inoffensive in an expression that only has a pejorative meaning. They would explain to a foreign tourist that the red-faced taxi driver who shouted 'get out of the road, you complete and utter pratt' is simply being friendly. This person I will call a *Nicer*. On the whole, they are well-meaning folk who palliate the stressed and impolite. Here is an (edited) example from the letters page of the *Bournemouth Echo*.

'Grockle' is not insulting

I came to this area 50 years ago... I found the word rather endearing and did not classify it as being derogatory or disparaging to our visitors from other areas.

Grockle is used in Dorset and south-west of England use to describe the out-of-towners that cause traffic queues, take up parking spaces, drop litter without paying the council tax to have it picked up, rant, rant, etc, etc. Grockle is loaded with resentment and envy of holidaymakers going to the beach when locals have to work. In short, grockle = bad, bad, bad. The nicer continued:

I therefore took the trouble to look up the meaning of the word. It would appear to be originally a French word meaning "nomadic" or "wanderer."

I cannot find grockle in any dictionary that I own. I have found references on the internet that are *slightly derisory*, *mildly derogatory* or *derogatory*. On the 'net, the *Oxford Dictionaries* website traces the first confirmed usage relating to tourists to the 1962 film, *The System*. Grockle was heard by the script-writer in Torquay during production and was used in the film, Because of this, grockle is thought to be a West Country dialect word. The first known appearance of any kind was in 1937 in issue no. 1 of

The Dandy in a comic strip called *Jimmy and His Grockle*. The letter concluded:

...I know that the hundreds of people whom I have heard use this word have never meant it in any insulting way towards the visitors...

Brian Jameson,
Gough Crescent, Poole

This correspondent's address is only a few hundred metres from where I was born and lived for the first 18 years of my life. Yet, I have only ever heard *grockle* used negatively and have yet to meet anyone with a different opinion. As the Manic Street Preachers put it: "This is my truth, you tell me yours." Two collective nouns for use in Dorset could be, *a hatred of tourists* and *a departure of grockles.*

In 2004, Britain dropped some of the items from the basket of goods that government statisticians use to compile the cost of living index. Out went gin, frozen turkey and local newspapers. In came mineral water, digital cameras, regional cheeses and acoustic guitars. This represents the changing lifestyles and social situations of the general population. I do wonder if certain old grumps would rather include typewriter ribbons and bottles of ink in the cost of living index.

Another issue is about the different meanings of similar words. *May* and *might, inquire* and *enquire, imply* and *infer* and *shall* and *will* are pairs of words were the distinction is becoming blurred. *Exactors* fight tooth and nail to retain the differences. Thanks to a rich and colourful history, English is rich in synonyms. However, the language would be all the poorer if differentiation is lost, especially as there are contexts where an exact sense is required to convey the meaning. For a great many people, though, the distinctions are unnecessary. A youth doesn't really care if a teacher infers or implies that last night's homework was cut and pasted from the internet. The point is whether they can get away with it. Compare that to a high profile divorce case seeking to apportion blame with the hope of financial gain.

Similar words can cause confusion. A building is on fire. There are two tanks of liquid outside; one marked *flammable* and the other *inflammable*. Which should a firefighter apply?
I was thinking of buying my wife a present for her birthday. Should I get her something *priceless* or *worthless*?

President Bush the Second referred to himself as the *decider*: "I'm the decider, and I decide what is best." Very quickly e-mails were being circulated about 'his decidership' and 'the decider-in-chief" because 'decider', in the sense of someone who makes decisions, is not universally recognised. This is grammar fascism at its worst. Someone who teaches is a teacher, a farm owner might be a farmer, and a person who plays golf is a golfer. English allows the nouns to be created in this way (could this process be called nouning?) We are quite used to making *a request* or *requesting* something. In the same way, to ask for something could be expressed as 'this is a big ask, but...' It will be coming to a page near you soon! The works of

Shakespeare and Chaucer showed a large number of words not previously recorded. These literary giants have a modern-day rival in the American satirist and wit, George W Bush.

An exactor wrote with typical fascist finality: "...for the last time, the word is oriented." The complaint here is about the word *orientated*. It is a bastardised version of *oriented* and, just as *preventive* is transposed into *preventative*, should not exist. This is an ostrich-like claim. Orientated turns up regularly in newspapers and should we then shorten *argumentative* to *argumentive*? My computer spellchecker did not reject orientated. I picked 2 online dictionaries at random. Orientated was represented in both. Surfing on my bookshelf, I consulted 3 good old-fashioned printed dictionaries, one each from Australia, Britain and the USA. Sure enough orientated was in all of them; existing as verb and adjective on the same page as its sister word, oriented. It is popular usage that determines what becomes accepted and understood. In this case, the dictionary compilers are doing their duty. My favourite dictionary gave 5 definitions. The first of these was 'to place as to face east.' Facing east we usually associate with religion, as in churches being aligned with the altar at the east end. This brings us back to faith. Those who would deny orientate do so purely as a matter of dogmatic belief, whereas it is a matter of personal choice. I have a preference. Do you? If we want to search and destroy words that we don't like, may I suggest intolerance, ignorance, pedantry, prejudice and sticklerism as well as the concepts that they describe.

Not all grammar fascists are negative. Indeed, some are very useful. When you need to know that the collective noun for a group of *dolphins* is a *pod* then you can be sure that an exactor will pop up to inform us all. Thanks to William Wordsworth we know there is *a host of golden daffodils* (is it different if they aren't golden, but a lighter shade of yellow?). If there really are such collective nouns as *a deceit of lapwings* and *a murder of crows,* then I suggest that we could borrow both of these for gatherings of grammar fascists. If we chose the latter, we will need a body of pathologists to word out whodunnit.

Crescendo is the process of growing louder so you can't actually reach it. Therefore, according to almost any dictionary you might care to consult, my use in the introduction is incorrect. However, the modern saying is *reaching a crescendo*; commonly known as the *peak of loudness.* No doubt, members of symphony orchestras preserve the formal meaning of the word as it is part of their professional vocabulary. The exactors cling to the dictionary definition just so that they have another axe to grind. But language is democratic in the sense that usage does not always bow to correctness. If a word, phrase or expression is suitable, it will be accepted. If it is accepted, it will be used. If enough people use it, it is. As a consequence, I would like it known that I approve of *all-day breakfasts* and *daily specials.*

9. Casting a spell

I don't give a damn for a man that can only spell a word one way.

Mark Twain

English spelling is katastrofic. The contribution of the languages that make up English, combined with the efforts of scholars to add their own spin, have left us with the legacy of orthography that is inconsistent to say the least. The vagaries of English allow grammar fascists to pounce on misspellings. I would suggest that instead of finding fault we look seriously and consider if English really is fit for purpose as a language.

Christian missionaries squeezed the phonemes (sounds) of Old English into 23 Latin letters plus a few extra that were made up to represent unusual (to the missionaries) pronunciations This evolved into the 26-letter English alphabet. There are 40 main phonemes, but only 26 letters. The biggest difficulty that most learners of English encounter is that there are so many instances where the written word does not appear on the page as it is spoken. A few examples: yacht, answer, palm, forehead, Wednesday. These words are usually pronounced: yot, anser, paam, forred and wensday (or even wedensday in parts of the north of England and Scotland). The question is whether we should speak as we write or spell as we speak. Or, of course, continue to accept that speech and spelling in English don't match on quite a number of occasions. Sometimes it is even difficult to make out a spelling from how a word is pronounced. An antique or a souvenir might be called a collectable, or is it collectible? Said in true British monotone mumbling, one has to listen very carefully to hear a difference. Which is the correct spelling, *collectable* or *collectible*? Some grammar fascists might insist on *-able* as the most suitable by falling back on a Latin precedent. However, the spellchecker accepts both, as do all of the dictionaries that I consulted.

Young people might say that the English language is gay. It certainly is bright and colourful. Not least because of homophones, homographs and homonyms. A homograph has the same spelling as another word, but a different meaning. A homophone has the same pronunciation as another word, but a different meaning. A homonym has the same pronunciation and spelling as another word, but a different meaning. A homograph that is pronounced differently is known as a heteronym. Please read the next three sentences carefully out loud.

Just for the record, I would like to record that I was not present when the row took place about which row to present first. I would like to minute that we should not close our eyes to the minute differences in terms of abuse that arise when we become close to a solution about the abuse of language. I mean that the mean level of mean abuse is too high for two people to deal with.

Did you sort out the homophones, homographs and homonyms? I shall just point out that the two *means* are both homophones and homographs. A

87

quarter of the world's population either speak, or are learning to speak, English. Honestly, why should anyone bother? When you learn English you have to learn everything 3 times. First you learn how to pronounce it, then you learn what it means, then you have to learn how to spell it, but not necessarily in that order!

We don't always need the correct spelling to understand. Recently, I received the following text in an e-mail for the umpteenth time since the internet began back in 1992:

Aoccdrnig to rscheearch at an Elingsh uinervtisy, it deosn't mttaer inwaht oredr the ltteers in a wrod are, the olny iprmoetnt tihng is taht the frist and lsat ltteers are in the rghit pclae. The rset can be a toatl mses and you can sitll raed it wouthit a porbelm. Tihs is bcuseae we do not raed ervey lteter by itslef but the wrod as a wlohe.

However, it is so much easier if the spellings follow patterns that we are used to. Americans prefer the theater, while Britons like to be at the centre. Spelling should not distract a reader from the content of writing. The main benefit of correct spelling to the reader is speed in reading. The only benefit to the writer, however, is to demonstrate willingness to conform.

There are times when the only acceptable spelling is the correct one. Despite being blamed for all manner of ills in the language, the internet proves the point. Anyone who has had a message from a 'mailer-demon' with the subject box marked "message returned - recipient unknown" has either made a spelling or a syntax mistake. An e-mail to john.smith@encyclopaediasrus.com might not be delivered for two reasons, the dot between john and smith and the mis-spelling of encyclopaedia. johnsmith@encyclopediasrus.com receives his mail with no problems. The same is true of www addresses. Type something incorrectly into the URL box and you either get an unwanted website or *Error 404 page not found* appears. In search engines you will be asked: "Do you mean encyclopediasrus?" As they have been programmed to recognise that we are either poor at spelling or, most likely, heavy-fingered on the keyboard and when no matches are found, they offer us an alternative.

Computers and the internet are subjects to which I shall return later. However there are two points that feel at home in this chapter. What should the software that is supposed to check and correct our spelling be called? Is it *spellchecker*, *spell checker*, a *spell-checker*, *spelling checker* or *spelling-checker*? The advice offered by the dictionaries in my collection varies. I can find all the above, but not all in the same dictionary[1]. My spell checker did not react to any of the optional spellings. None were marked as inappropriate. The computer even had no difficulty with spell chequer. Apart from the last spurious example, surely all are correct and we are free to choose. This then begs an

[1]I also discovered the role of dictionaries as history books. I have a 'contemporary' dictionary from 1987 that has no entry at all.

important question. Should a writer plump for one spelling and stick with it or put the variant that suits at the time of writing? Variation of this kind will annoy some, but delight others. Some claim that to use different spellings of the same word in one piece might show ignorance of what is correct. Kids in school often do this if they are unsure of a spelling. They repeat a word, but spell it differently in the hope that at least one will be acceptable. Others maintain that variation is the sign of a vibrant language. I wonder how many people actually notice the same word being spelled in different ways. I do. Sometimes I am annoyed, some times delighted. However, as long as I understand, I am never offended.

The second computer-related issue concerns the internet or is it the Internet? Is this a capital concern? A contemporary dictionary may be of some help.

The Simplified Spelling Society (SSS) has the aim of updating English spelling. The SSS says letters of the alphabet were designed to represent speech sounds. This allows a reader to pronounce words from the spellings, and a writer to spell them from the sounds. The society believes that as a result of historical development, English has lost its way and needs reform. The society has several suggestions as to how phonic English should work. Examples of more or less serious proposals to change English spelling include: Freespeling, New Spelling 90, Nuspelynh, NuEnglish, SoundSpel,Cut Spelling and Saaspel. Some of these ideas are not entirely dissimilar to Mark Twain's *A Plan for the Improvement of English Spelling.*

For example, in Year 1, that useless letter "c" would be dropped to be replased either by "k" or "s", and likewise "x" would no longer be part of the alphabet. The only kase in which "c" would be retained would be the "ch" formation, which will be dealt with later. Year 2 might reform "w" spelling, so that "which" and "one" would take the same konsonant, wile Year 3 might well abolish "y" replasing it with "i" and Iear 4 might fiks the "gj" anomali wonse and for all. Jenerally, then, the improvement would kontinue iear bai iear with Iear 5 doing awai with useless double konsonants, and Iears 6-12 or so modifaiing vowlz and the rimeining voist and unvoist konsonants. Bai Iear 15 or sou, it wud fainali bi posibl tu meik ius ov thi ridandant letez "c", "y" and "x" -- bai now jast a memori in the maindz ov ould doderez -- tu riplais "ch", "sh", and "th" rispektivli. Fainali, xen, aafte sam 20 iers ov orxogrefkl riform, wi wud hev a lojikl, kohirnt speling in ius xrewawt xe Ingliy-spiking werld.

Apart from the issues of how and when highlighted by Twain's example, two concerns about this kind of spelling reform come to mind. First, a generation of school children taught *NewSpell* (author's own coining) would experience difficulties in written communication with older generations. Also, future generations would have difficulty reading the body of English literature in the original from before the reform. Second, for spelling reform to be equitable and rational, consideration has to be given to different Englishes around the world. To whom would it be fair and logical?

Which variety of English should be the standard for the new spelling? The Prime Minister at the time of writing is a chap called Tony Blair. He often pronounces the short *i* sound as an *a* e.g. *benefats*, *offace* and *conservataves*. Does Mr Blair set a good example for a spelling system based on phonetics? Some years ago, a letter from a BBC presenter in *The Daily Telegraph* complained about the pronunciation of the day that follows Monday. Standard British pronunciation is t-useday. In Norfolk, and most of the United States, toosday is the preferred form. The natural pronunciation for a large number of English men and women in counties like Dorset and Wiltshire and cities such as Southampton, Portsmouth and the home of that very famous dictionary, Oxford, is *choosday*. Why? People know that when it comes to language questions, you most often have choice. So, British, American, Australian or why not even Geordie or Brizzle (Bristol)? Either a large number of people would be dissatisfied or each regional variation should adopt its own spelling, thereby defeating the purpose. Consider this question: How many syllables are there in England? Anyone attending an international match where the three lions are involved will have no doubt. Three, of course: *Ing - er - lund.*

In any case, people have already begun to write phonetically. Have you seen examples such as these: *should of* instead of *should have, your* instead of you're and *loose* instead of *lose.* On a market stall in East London stands the sign, "Mobile phones un-lock hear." Penultimately, this extract comes from a football message board used by supporters of AFC Bournemouth who spend a fair amount of time discussing literacy:

stanthevan   Posted on 22/6   23:00
subject: *if u karnt beet um join um*
wot as appind too the standud off inglush onn dis bord latterly und duz it reely matter

ryantraves   Posted on 22/6   23:18
subject: ***if u karnt beet um join um***
nar, i fink its alwite rele, as longas we undastand each ova den hoo cares?

For further proof that we are edging towards writing as we speak, visit Norwich and find a nice riverside pub called the Ribs of Beef. Examine the signage. Either the signwriter was paid in kind and had drunk his payment in full before putting paintbrush to sign or this indicates phonetic spelling: "Wines and Champagne Imported largers"

The luddite tendency of grammar fascism condemns all new ideas before they are given a fair hearing. Quillists and penists want to preserve a complicated orthographic system However, to regularise English spelling completely would be to take out all the individualisms and thereby remove the Englishness.

10. Comma gain?

Many writers profess great exactness in
punctuation, who never yet made a point.

George Prentice

This chapter could well be of interest to
apostropharians, the brave defenders our language
against the insertions of aberrant apostrophes.
Apostropharians are a group of like-minded but
disparate people who advocate a zero tolerance
approach to punctuation. It is appropriate here to
mention The Apostrophe Protection Society.
Hailing from Boston in Lincolnshire, their stated
aim is "preserving the correct use of this currently
much abused punctuation mark in all forms of text
written in the English language." But the
Apostrophe Protection Society are not grammar
fascists. Their web site makes clear. "We are aware
of the way the English language is evolving during
use, and do not intend any direct criticism of those
who have made the mistakes above. We are just
reminding all writers of English text, whether on
notices or in documents of any type, of the correct
usage of the apostrophe should you wish to put
right mistakes you may have inadvertently made."
Well done, you chaps! Perhaps we should make a
case for making the rules even simpler and making
the existence of such a group unnecessary.

The greatest source of annoyance to TAPS
(apart from being reduced to an abbreviation) and
in particular the people who misunderstand its
aims, is the greengrocer's apostrophe. In the
vegetable market close to New Street station in

Birmingham, I found *tomatoes, tomatoe's* and *tomato's*. Why? Perhaps the answer is that all greengrocers have cauliflower ears and therefore misunderstood their teachers at school when they explained the rule. The greengrocer's apostrophe has gained this name because so many greengrocers have experimented with the possibilities of the language. Has it not occurred to the apostropharians who decry this particularly British institution, that it could be an attempt to attract attention? Maybe it's a kind of commercial spelling, like Toys 'R' Us, Kwik Save or Spud-U-Like. Could it be that as supermarkets have become dominant in food retailing, the grocers are pointing out that they are green grocers as well as greengrocers? They sell fresh fruit and veg as opposed to the plastic-packed, modified-atmosphere, goodness-washed-out offerings of the supermarkets. Is the apostrophe question just a publicity stunt? Will the grammar fascists give them the benefit of the doubt? I doubt it. The very heart of the pedant's rage is that whoever got it wrong did so because they didn't understand the rule. Well, what about the third of the three variations of more than one tomato, *tomato's*?

The apostrophe has two main functions. The first is in a genitive phrase. For example, the shoes belonging to Mary are Mary's shoes. The second is to show that something has been left out in a shortened version. It's called contraction. *It's* is a contraction of *it is*. So *tomato's* is a contraction of *tomatoes,* the apostrophe shows the missing letter *e*. *Tomato's* is therefore allowable according to one of the 'rules' even if it is not strictly correct.

Apostropharians, assuming that the greengrocers got it wrong, have failed to realise that those cunning purveyors of five portions a day knew all along and have been kidding us with this little joke for years. There is even another alternative, for those texting a shopping list; pot8-0s. The alternative is to copy the company that sells baked parts of the *Solanum tuberosum* plant - surprisingly, a member of the nightshade family - and call them spuds. The name potato came to us via Spanish from the extinct *Taino* dialect of the *Arawak* Indian people in the West Indies. Just as colonisation wiped out this language, so the grammar fascists would eradicate perfectly good English from the vocabulary of small retailers.

This is as good a reason as any to revisit the supermarket. A couple of years ago, I went to the Harford Bridge branch of Tesco's on the outskirts of Norwich. I will relate this tale although the company would probably prefer me not to do so. Not perhaps because of the content, but because the corporate line is that the store should be called Tesco. The rival chain started by the Sainsbury family is known as Sainsbury's. Perhaps, if I continue to call it Tesco's, as I have done all my life and will continue to do as long as the company is prepared to take my money, the conglomerate might claim that it was not actually Tesco, but another store in my imagination. But I do have photos as proof. They were taken on the 5th November 2003 at 17.48. You can see them for yourself on the website for this book. Thank goodness for electronic date stamps on digital pictures. There were two signs in the store that interested me. One proclaimed *disney video's,* the other stated *great value c.d's.* I asked to see the manager. I was met by a young man who said that he was in charge of the section at that particular time. The following dialogue was enacted between myself, N, and the manager of the section at that time, abbreviated to MOTSATT.

N: What's that? (pointing to the great value sign)

MOTSATT: What's what?

N: The sign.

MOTSATT: The CD sign?

N   Yes.

MOTSATT: The CDs are great value because they are cheap.

N: Sorry that's not what I meant. What is the apostrophe for? (drawing an apostrophe with my finger in the air for emphasis)

MOTSATT: That's to show that there is more than one!

I pointed out, in as non-a-grammar-fascist-kind-of-way that I could manage, that it may just be that neither of the 2 signs were quite right. By the New Year, the signs had been replaced. However, it did take a while for the message to filter through to the rest of the country. On September 3rd, 2004 I snapped a sign at a large Tesco's outside of Newcastle-upon-Tyne that advertised *video's.* A quick check of the big four supermarkets in Norwich one Wednesday in late 2005 found only Morrisons (spelt without an apostrophe) still using

CD's and *video's* on signage, although only on some signs and not others.

According to the *Purdue University Online Writing Lab*, the apostrophe has three uses. One of these is to indicate certain plurals of lowercase letters. However, if we consult The Apostrophe Protection Society they inform us that "Apostrophes are **NEVER** ever used to denote plurals!" So who are we to believe?

Just as superfluous apostrophes are making guest appearances all over the place, they are also disappearing on some signs. *Mens* clothing in BHS and *MENS TOILETRIES* in Boots are two examples that I have noted. In the second case this makes absolute sense to me as an apostrophe would ruin the neat line of the letters written in upper case. So what? Anyone looking for a jacket or some aftershave is concerned with locating the product and surely isn't going to stand and mull over the lack of punctuation to the extent that the original purpose is forgotten. The signs locate the goods. They work. They communicate. We buy. Please consider this. You have just consumed a double vanilla choco mocca crème caramel cappuccino in a conveniently sized paper bucket from a well-known coffee company, with or without an apostrophe in its name. Most of these companies don't actually deal with their waste, but leave it to others to clean up. It is usually about 20 minutes after you have left the shop that your bladder indicates a need for a toilet, lavatory, loo, bathroom, restroom or comfort station (delete according to preference or degree of euphemism abhorrence). So you cast your eyes around. The Gentlemen's Toilets are labelled simply Gents. With no apostrophe this grammatical inconvenience must be boycotted. Being an apostropharian, you have little choice but to cross your legs and suffer in silence.

What is the correct use of the possessive apostrophe when a word ends in *s*? We might get the answer from the patron saint of punctuation. Sadly this particular sainthood is vacant. But I do hope that the Catholic Church might fill this gap by appointing one of the 17 Saint Jameses to the position. I am proposing one of the Jimmies because I think that the answer might lie there. While I am waiting for the beatification committee to consider the nomination, I shall employ St James and the London A-Z in the search for an answer. Because St James links some places in the capital with which I have had an association. First, take a trip to Liverpool Street Station and catch a local train to Maryland. On arrival, turn right outside the entrance and walk along Forest Road. Immediately before the Newham Maternity Hospital you will see *St. James' Road*. So the answer is to put an apostrophe after the *s*. However, the street sign at the northern end of the road says *St James' Road*. Now, return to Liverpool Street and take a number 48 bus to London Bridge Station. From here, there is a nice little train that goes around to Victoria via viaducts that lift the tracks above the inner city. There is a great view of south London. Take this train and get off at the first station, South Bermondsey. (You can go back and continue later when it has stopped raining.) You will probably be alone on the platform as the station is most used on match days for those going to football at Millwall's ground, the New Den. Anyway, turn right along Wilderton Road, take a dog-leg into Galleywall road and, at the end, turn left into Southwark Park Road. You are now in an area that locals call "the Blue". I always assumed that it was named after the pub called the Blue Anchor, but I never asked as I would reveal myself not to be from the locality. Anyway the 4th road on the left is *St James's Road*. So, an apostrophe and an additional -*s* is also OK. Now go back to London Bridge. From there, take a Caterham bound train to Kenley. Go out of the station to the main road and walk back towards Purley. The first road that you will come to is *St. James Road*. That is *St. James Road* with no apostrophe of any sort at all. Three London streets, three apostrophe options. Not only that, but there is disagreement over whether *St* or *St.* should be the abbreviation for *saint*. Oh, and St, James church after which the road is named is called *St James* on the sign, but *St. James'* on all the posters. We need divine intervention to sort it out. Oi, cardinals, hurry up and make that appointment.

Perhaps it is simply a matter of choice. During a report of a football match on *BBC Radio Solent*, a member of the Bournemouth team had been particularly active in playing the ball towards goal from the wing. In his match summary, the reporter used each of the following:

A Richard Hughes cross...
Richard Hughes's cross...
A cross by Richard Hughes...

So was the reporter varying his speech or was he demonstrating that he didn't know the rule about the apostrophe and tried all three versions in the hope that one of them would be correct. This leads on to a modest proposal. Why not abolish the genitive apostrophe? After all, we add an *-s* to show possession, so why an extra mark. If only it were that simple. The position of the apostrophe has the function of showing whether something is plural or singular. Compare *the boy's shoes* with *the boys' shoes*. So, on second thoughts, keep the apostrophe but *only* use it for plurals. The footwear example then becomes: the *boys shoes* and *the boys' shoes*. On third thoughts, there was a sign on a tower block in Stepney that read: "Tenants refuse to be put down the chute." The sign was supposed to mean: "Tenant's refuse to be put down the chute." The apostrophe shows the meaning of *refuse*. It meant *rubbish* rather than *say no*. As ever, the devil is in the detail. In order to simplify the use of the apostrophe other areas of English need to be examined. If there were quick and easy solutions to the complications in the language, they would surely have been applied, there would have been no grammar fascists and no books like *Eats, Roots & Leaves*. The real question is that if there is a desire to simplify English, is there a will to accept that change cannot be made without an overall view. The rules and conventions governing English is like a spider's web, with each segment dependent on other the strands. Break too many segments and the web ceases to be. There is no quick fix!

Whatever, the scale of the misuse of the genitive apostrophe may indicate that it has outlived its purpose. St James Road in Kenley is not confusing, unlike his namesakes' (or namesakes, namesake's or namesakes's) roads in Forest Gate and Bermondsey. The continued presence of this grubby little mark causes confusion to native speakers and learners of English alike. Would we miss it if it wasn't there in most situations? I think not. The *Bakers Oven* shop in Norwich would no longer be photographed by apos trophy hunters. Street sign writers, football reporters and greengrocers would then be beyond reproach. In the long term, English would be much better off without it. No genitive apostrophes = no complaints. So many other languages manage without it. Why can't we?

Now, if you are sitting comfortably, there is a punctuation question that concerns the same mark but this time as a subscript rather than superscript: To comma or not to comma? That is the question. Apart from mixed metaphors, this is one issue certain to ignite grammar fascists into blazing infernos of rage. Should a comma be used before the word *and* when making a list? The pro-comma brigade would write *lock, stock, and barrel,* while the anti-comma regiments would argue for *lock, stock and barrel.* The great thing is that you can do both. I have found that Americans tend to belong to the pros while the British are most often antis. I ran this through a computer spellchecker which liked the former until I switched to US English when it did a U-turn and plumped for the second version. Just to show that my assertion may not be true for all cases. The pro-comma and anti-comma lobbies will have to agree to differ on this issue. You can choose. The only difficulty is to be careful that you don't upset a grammar fascist who happens to hold the opposite belief. There is even a debate about what this particular comma should be called. Some call it the Oxford comma, others the Harvard comma. I, not being a great fan of branding, prefer to call it by the more generic name of serial comma. For the record; in their style manuals, the *Times*, *Guardian* and the *Australian Government* and most sources in the British English sphere of influence do not recommend this unnecessary slip of the pen or the third finger on the keyboard, while the Oxford University Press has, like the majority of American sources, pronounced its approval.

Lawyers have to be precise in their language. Many legal documents are written without commas to avoid any possible misunderstanding. Lord Denning, the High Court judge was notable for his short sentences. When delivering a judgment, he wanted no-one to be able to misinterpret what he had to say. After all, the problem with long sentences, and clauses separated by commas, is that they may start out in Dorset and end up in Hampshire as the ending has nothing to do with the beginning.

I read the following in a style guide concerning the use of the comma in dates: November 5th, 2007 is correct, but 5th November, 2007 is wrong. The reason given is that the comma divides the number. Yes, this is logical. Good that the first one is correct, but why should it make the second wrong? Why can't we have both? Try saying the two out loud. The space for pause before 2007 is exactly the same in both examples. So, why not have a comma there too? Creeping grammar fascism or a comma too far?

Of course it is the unwarranted presence of a comma that gives rise to the joke that lies behind the title of this book. The story is in the appendix

The Booker Prize-winning novel - *True History of the Kelly Gang* - contains no commas. The author, Peter Carey says: "They are a really useful instrument and you really don't want to throw them away." Another novel - *Dance of the Goblins* - by Jaq D Hawkins has not one semi-colon. During editing, a proof reader suggested that there were around 58 instances where a semi- colon could have been used. "I just don't like them," the author said and refused all changes on this issue. Can we argue? Should we bother? Hurrah for the Careys and the Hawkinses of this world!

11. Sorry?

> It is impossible for an Englishman to open his mouth without making some other Englishman hate or despise him.
>
> George Bernard Shaw

Pedants are actively concerned with many issues of spoken English. Two of these are discussed in this chapter and have been selected on the grounds that they relate to the twin themes of *Eats, Roots & Leaves*, the inconsistency of English and the intolerance of grammar fascists.

If it is difficult to decide how words should be spelt compared to how they are pronounced, it is an even harder task to work out how to pronounce words from spellings. The extent of complexity can be summed up in one word, *ough[1]*. It isn't a word at all, but an exclamation, that is, something that someone might say when they miss the nail with a hammer hit their nail instead. Some people might prefer to spell it ow! In which case, it is a word. *The Oxford English Dictionary* lists ow as exclamation, expressing sudden pain. But I don't mean to refer to *ough* on its own as it doesn't get an entry in the *OED*. Please look at this list of words and either say them out loud or imagine doing so.

though, although, furlough, dough
thought, brought, ought, wrought, sought, nought
borough, thorough
dough,
rough, tough, enough
drought, plough

hiccough
lough

There are eight sets of words containing *ough*, each having its own pronunciation. There is a bit of cheating going on here. The last in the list, pronounced loch, is Anglo-Irish for a lake. It could be argued, and some will argue, even if only for the sake of argument, that it isn't a proper English word. But lough arrived in Middle English from Ireland and, having been around for at least 500 years, must be counted. The cheat is number seven. It is pronounced hiccup. The spelling, *hiccough,* arose because it became by associated with cough. A hiccough is, according to the *OED*: "an involuntary spasm of the diaphragm and respiratory organs, with a sudden closure of the glottis and a characteristic gulping sound." Hiccough has absolutely nothing to do with coughing. Because of this false etymology, some maintain that hiccough isn't a proper word. Collins dictionary says it was first used in the 16th century and it is in each and every one of the dictionaries on my shelf. This might seem like a long digression from discussing the *ough* sound, but I can explain. As hiccough was derived from hiccup, it is a valid alternative. However, there are those who insist that the only correct spelling of the word for the involuntary diaphragm spasm, pronounced hiccup,

[1]*The Urban Dictionary* of slang on the internet lists *ough*: "When said, something is shocking, in a good way." *(Ralph gets a 50 yard goal in Fifa 2005) "Oooouuugh!"*

is *hiccough*. This is another piece of grammar fascistery. Irregardless of whether you accept 6 or 8 pronunciations of ough, the fact remains that learning how to speak English from the written word is not an easy task.

British spoken English contains so much more information than just the message conveyed. There is great variation in the pronunciation around the British Isles. Many of these are well-known, such as the long or short *a* sound that varies from north to south in such words as *bath*.

It is less widely understood that we can distinguish class and religion from how words are pronounced and the vocabulary used.

Taking vocabulary first, social class can most often be identified by choice of words for an item or concept. What is the item of furniture called that more than one person can sit on in a living room? Working class people invariably say *settee*, middle class people say *sofa*. A third option *couch* is used by both classes. What are midday and evening meals called? *Dinner* and *tea* are working class. *Lunch* and *dinner* are middle class. Of course these are tendencies rather than absolutes. They become interesting when misunderstandings occur. This is especially difficult for non-native speakers of English. The Swedish translator working on an early episode of the Australian TV programme, *The Flying Doctors,* misinterpreted the meaning of evening meal. "I'll put the tea on," meaning 'I shall prepare food,' was translated as 'I will make you a cup of tea.' This was made all the more obvious as the speaker in the scene had just poured everyone a beer.

It is an over generalisation, but no other variety of English can define class by the vocabulary as well as British. Class, or perhaps we should rather say education nowadays, can be heard in pronunciation. The word *often* is a good marker. Working class people tend to pronounce the t. Middle class people do not; often is pronounced *offen*. Upper middle class and the aristocracy have a pronunciation that resembles a completely different word, *orphan*. It does not matter which pronunciation you have or choose, you should recognise a particularly insidious kind of grammar fascism that will judge your acceptability as a person on the way you speak. For me the term *class trip* used to mean when the teacher took us on an outing from school. Now it has acquired an additional personal meaning. Having gone to university and become a teacher, I first unlearned the working class indictors of speech that distinguished me from most of my contemporary students. Then I re-learned them as I realised that adaptation of my speech pattern could have advantages. At professional conferences I would use middle class articulation and vocabulary. At school, in one of the most deprived areas of London, I would talk to the pupils in a way that was not alien to them. It can be very important to show that one that one belongs.

I have not only the luxury of having more than one way to speak, but also experienced a phenomenon of language change at first hand. *Estuary English* is the term now applied to a composite way of speaking that has emerged. In brief, it is a mixture of two types of speech. One is the upper and middle class pronunciation that is used by, amongst others, the British royal family. It is known as Received Pronunciation or RP or what was once called 'posh.' RP used to be synonymous with BBC English as it was once the only type of English that was thought suitable for broadcast. The second part of this new kind of speech is Cockney, the working class dialect of London. Some people see it as a levelling out of *sociolects* (dialect according to class or social standing). Grammar fascists see it as another glottal stop closer to the end of the line for English. It can be argued that it contains more working class Cockney than upper class Received Pronunciation. For this reason, grammar fascists look upon the use of Estuary English as vulgarising the language. They use such a description because, being language snobs, they regard Cockney as being of low status and inferior. Estuary English is so called because it was first identified around London. The estuary is the Thames. I do not intend to describe Estuary English any further. A great deal has already been published about it. But I will highlight just one aspect. *Cheers* is an exclamation expressing good wishes before taking a drink. In Estuary, it has two other meanings that have come from Cockney. It may mean thank you: 'Cheers for that.' Cheers can also mean goodbye: 'See you on Sunday then, cheers.' Both of these greatly annoy grammar fascists. Cheers for that!

I have often (in which I always voice the *t*) been questioned rather closely when I have stated that it is even possible to distinguish which church a person might attend depending on the pattern of speech. In Northern Ireland there is the well-known h shibboleth. Protestant schools teach *aitch* and Catholics learn *haitch*. As almost everyone in Ulster attends a denominational school, the pronunciation of the letter between *g* and *i*, can determine religious affinity to a very high degree. An easier way to find out is to ask the name of the second-largest city in the province. Catholics invariably say Derry, Protestants call it Londonderry. This can be explained more as a political choice rather than decided by education. Your choice of what to call the city, may indicate taking sides in some people's eyes. Road signs are continuously vandalised with the *London* half of *Londonderry* painted out and in by activists. The BBC local radio station avoids the issue by being called Radio Foyle. The maiden city as it is also known, has also become referred to as Stroke City. The latter comes from BBC presenter, Gerry Anderson, who said "Derry-stroke-Londonderry" on air as a diplomatic compromise. This became shortened to Stroke City. However, the search for a term that upsets no-one appears to please nobody.

There are also denominational schools in Liverpool and there is a shibboleth concerning the sound of the word *early*. The two main songwriters in the Beatles each went to a church school. John Lennon attended a Roman Catholic school and said *airly*. Paul McCartney went to a Church of England school and therefore says *urley*. In Glasgow all you have to do is find out whether the affinity is for Celtic or Rangers in football. I would advise against answering the question yourself, unless you are completely sure that your response is the one approved of by the questioner. In England grammar fascists will identify your origin or class by your speech. In Scotland's largest city, to make a choice between the two Old Firm teams, could even assign you to hospital.

Inconsistency in English means that there are different ways of saying the same thing. Where differences become apparent in language, there will be controversy, which is a controversy in itself. Here is a selection of the issues that cause dilemmas.

controversy: is the stress on the 1st or the 3rd syllable?

dilemma: is the *di* like in did or died?

ate: should it rhyme with 8 or met?

economic: does the *e* resemble the e sound of *egg* or *Easter?*

medicine: has it 2 syllables (med-sin) or 3 (med-i-sin)?

trait: is the final -t pronounced or not?

I shall be prescriptive and say that there is only one answer in each case. That is to pronounce the word in whichever way you wish and don't let anyone else say that your pronunciation is incorrect. Although do be prepared that you will be judged on your speech.

A discussion about where to place the stress in English words ran for several days in the letters page of *The Guardian*. I can summarise the various contributions thus: "Pennine may be a *trochee* or a *spondee* depending on whether you are measuring it as a modern English word with the stress on the first syllable, or as a classical Greek word with a longer vowel sound in the second syllable. Pencil is much more clearly a trochee in which the first syllable is stressed much more than the second; pen top is much more clearly a spondee where the two syllables have equal weight. Pennine is in between. There is a drop in stress, so that you could call it a trochee, but it is so slight that spondee could apply."

Unlike most letters sent to newspapers about English, this discussion had none of the hallmarks of squabbling grammar fascists. There is a great difference between those who use their command of English in an attempt to defeat opponents and those who use their depth of knowledge to enlighten others. Thanks to correspondents in Cambridge, Manchester, Surrey and Scotland, I now know what to call a word with stress on the first syllable and a word with equal stress on the first and second syllables. And so do you!

There is a trend in spoken English that annoys certain grammar fascists. This has various names: upspeak, uptalk and HRT (high-rising terminals) where the tone of voice goes up at the end of a sentence and makes a statement sound like a question. A pilot on a QANTAS airliner said: "We shall be climbing to a height of 11,000 metres?" and "We are now at our cruising speed of 825 kmh?" as if he were asking us, the passengers! It is particularly noticeable in the Englishes spoken in New Zealand, Australia, California, Canada and Northern Ireland. It is now spreading amongst young people in the rest of Britain. According to David Crystal, women use it twice as much as men, teenagers 10 times as much as others and working class people 3 times as much as middle class. Without invoking a stereotype, if you would like to hear this for yourself, the statistics suggest that you could listen to the speech of young, female shop assistants. A great many people are uncomfortable with this new development in English. As you might expect, the wooden-headed grammar fascist has an opinion which, I hasten to add, I do not share. His words of tolerance and understanding shall close this chapter: "I hate upspeak."

12. CUL8R

Why don't you all f-fade away
And don't try to dig what we all s-s-say
I'm not trying to cause a big s-s-sensation
I'm just talkin' bout my g-g-g-generation

Pete Townshend

Society is in constant change. The Romans could not have foreseen a world of electric and electronic communication. Even the soothsayers and mystics which were very much part of Roman life could not have predicted our modern world. They had no idea. The Romans had no number for zero. Devoid of zeros, there could be no decimal system. Being short of a 0 to go with a 1 would mean no binary system. Without a binary system, there would be no computers and consequently neither e-mail nor mobile phones. The lack of the concept of a number representing nothing was bound to mean that Roman communication was destined to amount to nought. We live in an electronic age and English has adapted to keep pace with developments. The first electric communication required a new form of English too. That was provided by Samuel Morse in the form of the dots and dashes that make up the code used for telegraph and early radio communication. This was an entirely new way of representing the language so that messages could be transmitted.

Few will likely come into contact with Morse code, but the vast majority in the western world have access to the changing forms of English that have adapted to modern information and communications technology. Melvyn Bragg said: "The whole thing about punctuation and language as a whole is that we know it will change." Mobile phones have provided us with SMS - the short message service. As the name suggests, SMS allows us to send a short note of up to 160 characters from one mobile phone to another. This means apart from a cheap way to get a message across and the fact that we can leave it without having to suffer a reply or a long phone call. For example, I'm told that dumping boyfriends and girlfriends by text is almost the only way to do it in Croydon. Text messaging will change the language. When enough people know what these abbreviated words mean they will infiltrate the language and enter dictionaries. Barclays Bank ran a newspaper advert with a picture of a mobile phone showing the message: "In case u 4get, B'card wl txtyou a bill repayment reminder." The Emmanuel Baptist Church in Swanage, Dorset had a poster outside that read: "With God UR never the weakest link." Text messaging reached the mainstream.

On the 3rd of March 2003, the *London Evening Standard* published an article about an essay reputedly written by a schoolgirl in Scotland. The essay was presumably of the "what I did on my summer holidays" type and read:

"My smmr hols wr CWOT. B4 we usd 2go2 NY 2C my bro, his GF & thr 3 :-kids FTF. ILNY, it's a gr8 plc."

This can be translated into more standard English as:

My summer holidays were a complete waste of time. Before, we used to go to New York to see my brother, his girlfriend and their three screaming kids face to face. I love New York. It's a great place.

However, this is quite probably an urban legend. The "essay" is too well written, as if to show off how clever one can be with text language. I could not imagine any schoolgirl using such a sophisticated turn of phrase as face to face. This phrase is anyway superfluous to the story as it is already explained by *2C* and the point about text messaging is that it is as brief as possible. Absolutely certain is that no member of the thumb tribes would bother with the apostrophe in *it's*. Also, this essay would have been handed in to the teacher at the beginning of the new term in September and would have been far too newsworthy to take six months to reach the newspapers. Further, the article said that the Scottish Qualifications Authority (the body responsible for school exams in Scotland) expressed its concerns in a report that said: "Text messaging was inappropriately used" in an English exam. School examinations take place in late May and June, so this essay couldn't be the one that they were talking about. I believe that the newspaper story, as much as the essay itself, is a work of fiction! I call this the Great Text Message Hoax and will continue to do so until I see proof to the contrary. The purpose of the article was that some youngsters are using text message shorthand in areas other than on a mobile phone, but perhaps had a more extreme intention that is dealt with later in this chapter.

The GTMH, however, does provide us with a modern-day Rosetta Stone where texting meets English.

The internet is another area where English has a form noted for its brevity. Chatting is a strange way to describe a form of communication that is actually written down. Although it is people sitting at keyboards contributing to a discussion in real time, it isn't quite the same as a conversation. In speech we get face-to-face interaction that gives immediate feedback. In chatting you have to wait for someone to finish typing and press enter before you can reply. In a conversation you can interrupt a speaker or show through facial expression signs of agreement or disapproval. All this is missing in chatting. Also unlike a discussion, 30 people can monitor and contribute to a discussion simultaneously. Imagine trying to listen and respond to a group that large if they were all speaking at once! The rhythm, variations of speed and pitch (perhaps thankfully, hesitations such as err and um[1]) are absent in chatting, so people invent conventions to express actions. When a phrase appears in purple between asterisks it denotes an action e.g. *listens to grammar fascist on radio*. Feelings are expressed with the aptly named symbols called *emoticons* that are also known as *smileys* e.g. ;-), :-O. In chatting, speed is of the essence. Capital letters are dropped, most punctuation is omitted and commonly used phrases are abbreviated; *idk*, *btw*, and *imo* mean respectively *I don't know*, *by the way* and *in my opinion*. There are hundreds of TLAs (three letter acronyms) in use, despite the fact that they aren't acronyms and many have more or less than 3 letters. Quillists and penists might maintain that chatting conventions are just laziness or that the vast majority of internet users are one or two finger typists. Capital letters are sometimes used. The phrase, LOL (laughs out loud), is typed to let others know that you found something humorous. This has hyperbolic forms, ROFL, meaning 'rolls on the floor laughing' and ROFLMAO 'rolls on the floor laughing my ass off.' When I first discovered chatting I was surprised by the LOLs and how people in a chat room might compete to see who could laugh in the most extreme way. One day, after a few ROFLs and ROFLMAOs I typed: ILSMIFOMCAHMHOTD. Immediately the screen was flooded with question marks; a sign that an explanation is called for. Others wanted to know about this abbreviation as it isn't a standard TLA. I explained: "I laughed so much I fell off my chair and hit my head on the desk." Needless to say, it hasn't caught on.

E-mail is another area where English has adapted to a new medium of communication. An e-mail is not an electronic letter. They don't usually begin with *Dear* and end with *yours anything* as a paper letter might. Importantly, the text of the original message along with the exact time that it was sent appear on the screen when you reply to an e-mail. This makes 'in reference to your letter of the 23rd' and other such phrases superfluous. You can get straight to the point. Mails are often informal.

[1]Although people wouldn't normally bother to type these in, they appear when people mimic speech for dramatic effect.

One quickly goes to first name terms and the phrase 'to whom it may concern' is redundant in the sphere of e-mail. Of course no self-respecting grammar fascist would admit to testing or owning a computer. Indeed, the provisional wing of the quillists might expel a member for wilful possession of a typewriter with intent to cause actual bibliographical harm. If any stick-in-the-muds did venture into e-mailing they would find two terms of interest, cc and bcc. When you copy a mail to someone you type the address in the *cc box*. If you don't want the other person to see that you have copied the letter, you use the *bcc box*. These terms stand for *carbon copy* and *blind carbon copy* respectively. New technology has taken terms from the old. This isn't unusual in English. If you take a flight, you will *board*, enter *the cabin* and *stow* your luggage, all using terms borrowed from travel by ship. Why invent completely new expressions when there is perfectly good language available. English is good at recycling, especially as some new words don't catch on. The idea that the internet would bring people closer in net communities spawned such as *netizen*, *netspeak* and *netiquette*. Only the latter has any kind of common use as a convention of online politeness.

As the average age of internet users increases so use of English on the 'net is becoming more conservative, the geeks have given way to the silver surfers. Third-agers learnt their English in post-war society. Teenagers have scant k telephones and refrigerators were luxuries and mobile phones two generations in the future. Likewise, the intolerant oldies blame youth for corrupting and deconstructing English. As the language police cannot accept that society and consequently language must change, they round up the usual suspects, schools, teachers and young people.

Slanguage is part of what grammar fascists see as decline in English. If you don't like slang, don't use it. But that is no reason to criticise others for it. After all, language is a matter of choice. As long as we all understand one another there is no real harm done. This headline appeared in one British broadsheet:nowledge of this generation's upbringing when TV was rare,

English exam hit by epidemic of street language

Apart from the question of whether an exam can be hit by an epidemic, what was the story behind this hyperbolic headline? 'A report by the Edexcel exam board said there was "a surprising number of lapses" in Standard English.' Does "a surprising number" constitute an epidemic? Or is this just another grammar fascist complaint about young people? The article noted the use of words such as: *Gonna, m8, ain't, wanna, u, shouda* and *i* instead of *going to, mate, not, want to, you, should have* and *I* respectively. Instead of the "shock, horror" nature of the article, perhaps there is a greater issue to consider. For some school students to manage to write an essay of any kind represents a huge achievement. Anyone that has taught in a secondary school will know that there are some 15-year-olds who are not very able when it comes to writing skills. That they mange to express themselves in, most probably, the only area of

English that they have mastered should be celebrated rather than belittled. Of course, the highest standard of English should be encouraged and use of so-called street language is out of context and therefore is inappropriate. However, using text and chat language shows initiative in attempting to complete a task that would otherwise be too difficult.

In 2003, a grammar fascist complained about "crimes against the English language." In 2006 at the Professional Association of Teachers conference, delegates moaned that *Dick & Dom*, the favourite programme among 6 to 12- year-olds, undermines attempts to maintain standards of spoken English. A retired teacher complained of "fast, loud speech" where "all the words run into one and cannot be understood." Instead of saying *yes* and *no,* presenters said *yeah* and *nah*. What she meant was that she didn't like it. She also demonstrated how hopelessly out of touch she is. Her critique smacked of reverse ageism; 'it wasn't like that in my day.' Exactly. Whenever her day was, it is long gone. Criticism of young people's speech patterns I call *olditude*. Here's a message for the PAT. Children's TV is not designed for adults. You aren't meant to understand it. You certainly aren't meant to enjoy it. You aren't even expected to be watching it. A judge in the High Court, Mr Justice Lewison, likened rap lyrics to "a foreign language." Mr Lewison and PAT members might need to extend their linguistic skills.

If you overhear teenagers or even sub-teens beginning sentences: 'So she goes...' and 'she went...' you will be quick to understand that there is no travel or movement involved. The teens and tweens are using both of these expressions instead of *she said*. Imagine eavesdropping on a young person describing a dialogue between two teenagers:

So he went: "Whatever"
And she goes: "Am I bothered"
And he went: "Yeah!"
So she goes: "YEAH!"
You know what I'm saying?

Grammar fascists probably don't know what is being said and would indeed be bothered by what they would see as debasement of English. They may even have a valid point here, but both the speaker and those for whom the dialogue is intended know exactly what is being said. In a private conversation (even one at high volume that gives half the people in the high street access to it) surely any form of expression is allowable. There is another way that young people represent *said:* 'she was like...' There is no "crime" against the language here. My only regret is the lack of variation in expression and my hope is that young people have alternative ways of expression in other, more formal situations.

Discussing street language, abbreviated English and youthspeak, you might think should be under the heading slang. Slanguage is not the issue here. For what is, or is not, classed as slang is very much a personal judgement that varies with age, location and social class. There is also the widely-held assumption that slang can only ever be bad. In

October 2005, *The Observer* reported: "Teen writing improves as slang grows." The article quoted a report from Cambridge University that showed that Britain's school-leavers are more literate than at any time over the past 25 years. "Today's teenagers are using far more complex sentence structures, a wider vocabulary and a more accurate use of capital letters and punctuation..." The report also noted that although informal language is on the increase, it is still a small proportion of the total used. This kicks two major grammar fascist claims into touch. First the standard of literacy in schools is not declining. Second that slanguage is not rampant. Could it even be that the 'epidemic of street language' has helped school pupils become more literate?

One reservation about young people is the way some use the internet to acquiring knowledge about language. Speaking a language is a life-long learning process that is never complete. There will always be different ways of expression and new things to discover. There are those who subscribe to the 'click and know' philosophy. This is the belief that knowledge can be gained in one hit by copying and pasting in. The purposes of language were outlined in the introduction and for knowledge about language to be valid it has to be applied. That is, we have to use it. There is also the question as to whether websites can be relied upon. As I shall show later, there is information on the internet about English that is simply not true. I advise people to beware of the internet for very good reasons.

Youth can be blamed for many things, but they should be given credit for one thing. They have taken control of their own language. They don't speak my English, but *a big up*[1] to them for not conforming.

[1]To big up means to give respect, applaud, congratulate or acknowledge.

14. Triskaidekaphobia

It takes only one drink to get me drunk. The trouble is I can't remember if it's the thirteenth or the fourteenth.

George Burns

Someone who suffers from *triskaidekaphobia* has an irrational fear of, or avoids, the number 13[1]. There are people who stay in bed from the 12th to the 14th of any month, especially when the day to be avoided falls on a Friday. I have omitted chapter 13 to show understanding for the trepidation that some people experience. I would also like to express some solidarity with people who resent one of the widespread uses of language in our visual media.

A contents page showing the numbers of the chapters is simply a list. I know that there are many people who have been plagued by the current phenomenon of the list. A Sunday supplement is not complete without at least one list, 'the 10 must-have apple varieties for the autumn.' Or, for redtop readers who seem oblivious to the hyperbolic, 'the top 20 most-evil soap villains of all time.'' We have list programmes on TV, 'the 50 most-loved house makeover programmes as voted for by you the viewers.' I have something against lists too. They are always round numbers. Why not 'the 9 greatest celebrity chefs who have never upset another

[1] the word triskaidekaphobia itself may be considered safe for triskadekaphobes as it literally means 'three and ten fear.' I am just waiting for the e-mail to tell me that there is a word for the fear of word that describes fear of the number 13.

celebrity chef' (this list probably wouldn't even stretch to 9). Why are lists always some multiple of 10? What if you can't think of as many as 10 to make up a list or happen to come up with 11 items? In keeping with the idea of freedom to use the language, I see lists of 10 as a kind of tyranny: A sinister plot to decimalise the ordering of our thought. I am going to break with this attempt at dictatorship and have a list of 4.

The reason that this book has no chapter 13 is to show respect for those people who:

a) Refuse to travel on Friday 13th. The 33rd President of the United States[2], Franklin D Roosevelt, would delay his departure until a few minutes into Saturday the 14th. If you want to get a rather cheap flight in America, try to fly on the day that many try to avoid. The airlines dump the prices to compensate for the shortfall in passenger numbers when the 13th falls on a Friday.
b) Renumber their houses 11A or even 11½ - there is such a house numbered 11½ in Spitalfields, London, close to Liverpool Street station.

[2] Or was FDR only the 32nd? In 1884, Grover Cleveland was elected the 22nd president. Four years later he lost to Benjamin Harrison, who became the 23rd president. In 1892, Cleveland defeated Harrison. Was Cleveland the 24th president or was he still the 22nd? Grover Cleveland was one man, but is counted as two presidents. The man living in the White House for the moment is either the 43rd or 44th, depending on how you look upon Grover Cleveland. The choice is yours. Unless you are Michael Moore and you believe that the 43rd or 44th President of the USA is Al Gore.

c) Will actually pay someone to be the 14th dinner guest - apparently Mark Twain's triskaidekaphobia originates from when he was the 13th dinner guest and the food ran out[3].

d) Won't even utter the word for the number that follows 12. Somewhere between 1 in 8 and 1 in 12 people in the English-speaking countries suffer from a degree of triskaidekaphobia. What a shame that the statistic couldn't be 1 in 13, although, rounded up to the nearest whole number, 1 in 8 as a percentage is 13%!

As well as a pathological hatred of numbered lists (lists invariably avoid writing "proper" sentences with subject, verb and object), grammar fascists will no doubt complain that the table of contents has a number missing from the sequence. They will be furious at spoiling the logic and disturbing the continuity. But there is a completely different logic at work around the baker's dozen.

I was in line[4], waiting to check into the Comfort Hotel in Chicago. In front of me, a slightly heated discussion was taking place. A lady was attempting to get the intern[5] acting as clerk[6] behind the desk to understand why she could not accept room number 1411.

[3] Samuel Clemens has another numerical claim to fame besides his triskaidekaphobia. He got his pen name from the cry given out by the boys who would check for a safe depth of the river with sounding lines. "Mark Twain" meant at least 2 fathoms of water.
[4] queue [5] trainee [6] receptionist for British readers

I eavesdropped part of the conversation.

Intern:	Madam, as I have explained, this hotel does not have a 13th floor
Woman:	Exactly. As there is no 13th floor, then the 14th floor is the 13th floor!

I wondered if any hotel could have more than 12 floors or whether the top floors somehow floated above the 12th as they would surely collapse without the 13th floor. The point here is that the fear of the number 13 restricts the use of language.

People go to great lengths not to have any contact, linguistic or otherwise, with 13 and in certain circumstances might choose their words very carefully. This harks back to the days when people would not mention anything to do with the devil as there was a belief that by uttering his name he would be summoned and wreak havoc. This superstition still surfaces in modern day English. The arrival of the very person being talked about in a conversation is met with the remark "talk of the devil". These superstitions persist. On the Isle of Portland in Dorset, many people avoid saying the word rabbit.

Unlike the two triskaidekaphobes mentioned above, as well as Napoleon and another American president, Herbert Hoover, you have no worries about the number 13. I am actually pretty certain not to have offended anyone, as true triskaidekaphobics sharing the view of the lady in Chicago, have skipped this chapter and gone straight onto chapter 15. As Roosevelt might have said: 'We have nothing to fear, but fear itself, oh, and the number 13.'

You might have asked or you may now be asking yourself: "What does triskaidekaphobia have to do with grammar fascism?" Well, there are three possible answers (I couldn't think of 10). First, chapters 2 & 3 raised questions about some of the deeply held beliefs of the grammar fascists. Some of the supposed rules were shown to be half-truths and misunderstandings at best. At worst, some of the commandments carved in stone turned out to be little more than superstitions. So, a chapter about superstition is required to show that strange beliefs give rise to weird behaviour. This is it! Second, the title of the chapter demonstrates the complexity of English as the first parts *tris*, *kai* and *deka* are from Greek and *phobia* is from Latin. Grammar fascists will, of course, already know this as a result of all those long train journeys and would take great joy in pointing it out to anyone who may show enthusiasm anything above the level of disinterested. Third, *Grammarphiliacs* cannot but help falling in love with long words, especially those which require a little thought to be able to work out how to pronounce them. Triskaidekaphobia is such a long word with enough syllables to satisfy the smugness of someone who knows not only that there are seven different pronunciations of the letters *ough*, but is able to list them without being prompted.

I should like to point out a little grammar fascist tendency myself here. I began my three reasons with the words, first, second and third. This is correct. However, in the vernacular most would say, and probably write, the ordinal numbers as firstly, secondly, thirdly. Firstly, according to the *Oxford English Dictionary* is an adverb. So this usage must be wrong. First, I have no problem with this. Second, I don't believe that it is wrong. If so many people do add -*ly* then surely by common use it will become acceptable. Third, I choose not to follow the crowd on this issue.

Thus far in this chapter, I have avoided certain subjects. I could have introduced a discussion about when a number should be written as numerals or letters. Should it be 13 or thirteen? Should there be commas in large numbers such as 1,456,342? Should Americans be allowed to say *thousand forty-five* without the word *and* after thousand? These are matters where some people would like to enforce rules. I have opinions on all three, but the prospect of a spin-off book makes me follow my publisher's advice and remain tight-lipped. The decimal point is another area where people behave strangely with figures. Consider these two numbers, *0.5* and *5.0*. Now think about how we pronounce the 0. Usually it changes depending on its position relative to the decimal point. *Nought point five* is the usual way of saying the former. The latter, on the other hand, would rarely be *five point nought*. It would more likely be *five point o* or possibly even *five point zero*. But the important point is we have the freedom to say *o, zero* or *nought* when we speak of numbers. All three are acceptable, unless you are an airline pilot. Then zero is required for clarity of communication.

I won't avoid the inconsistency concerning numbers where words change their spelling depending on whether there is one or more. One foot is less than six feet. Unless someone happens to be six foot tall, or a yacht is fifty foot long; a fifty footer. In The Fens there are watercourses called Sixteen Foot Drain and Forty Foot River. Let the pedants produce a rule, with all the exceptions, for this issue. But of course, it's the charm of English that is important here. And it is the charisma of the language that helps us to resist all that European nonsense about metrication. No-one is going to climb a mountain and say: "I can see for kilometres." This is the thin end of the wedge. Give 'em an inch and they'll take 0.9144 metres!

Plurals can be straightforward or troublesome. But they certainly can get some people thinking. Take this correspondent for example;

... But surely the plural of "Father Christmas" should be Fathers Christmas"
John Lodge
London

There are quite a few words that don't actually seem to have a singular. Names of instruments such as: pliers, scissors, shears and jeans, pants, and tights. Both these categories have something in common. They are all one thing that has two parts. There is also the more difficult category of words ending in -ics which may or may not take a plural verb. Such words used strictly for the name of a discipline are regarded as singular: Economics, Ethics.

While we are on the subject of numerical inconsistencies, there is something else that I would like to single out. That is the word *couple*. This word means any amount up to about 20. Imagine that a friend says to you in the pub: "I left my wallet at home, can you lend me a couple of quid to buy my round." They would give you a very strange look if you thrust your hand into your pocket and fished up two pounds. So how many is a couple in this case? If there are five in your party, I would guess anything up to about a score. Not to change the subject from words that used to mean 2: A pair of shoes means two items, a pair of trousers means one. Don't you just love the logic of numerology in English? An older word for two of something is brace. How many, then, in a pair of braces?

Moving on from the terrible twos, we come to a threesome. Just a few years back, I was giving a lecture about American English. I said that when Americans repeat a repeat, i.e. they do something three times, there is a special word for it, *three-peat*, sometimes written *3-peat*. People didn't believe me until I showed them photographic evidence, a picture of an LA Lakers jacket celebrating three consecutive basketball championships and containing that word. I also showed a photo that I took of a caption to a sports programme on TV where Tiger Woods was up for a three-peat of some golfing trophy. Having proved the point, I was asked what follows a three-peat. I suggested four-peat and a double-double. A member of the audience suggested *quat-row*. I asked where he got the inspiration and he said the Audi Quattro

- a four-wheel drive car. *Quat* for *four* and *row* for in a *row*. The audience laughed and we all thought it a clever innovation, but that it would never catch on. Afterwards, I did a little research. *The Los Angeles Business Journal* reported: "As the Lakers charge into the playoffs, an entrepreneurial fan is getting into the game." The article continued: "Local graphic artist Jerry Leibowitz, 54, owns the copyright to "Quat-Row," a phrase he invented for describing a team that wins four straight championships" "I just hated four-peat." Leibowitz said. "It didn't make any sense phonetically."

There is an old saying "strange things happen at sea." Now that our Navy is only large enough to defend the Isle of Dogs and our merchant fleet is reduced to a couple of Dover Ferries and we have succumbed to the linguistic influence of Hollywood. Perhaps we should say "strange things happen in Los Angeles!" I have some more to say on this in chapter 19 (for grammar fascists qv ch. 19).

Some collective words imply certain group activities, e.g. golfers would recognise twosome, threesome, foursome as would people in certain intimate situations. Musicians would understand solo, duet, trio, quartet, etc. We would usually assume that twins, triplets and quadruplets were once wombmates.

While on the subject of more than one of something. In English, we simply add an –s, don't we? Of course the much-hated rhetorical, tag question *don't we?* is there because, mostly, we do. But there are exceptions. I can put a sock on my left *foot*. But I put two socks on my *feet*. There is one *man*, but two *men*, one *mouse* but several *mice*, one *child* but a crowd of *children*. You can cut the atmosphere with a *knife*, but if two people had the same idea they would need two *knives*. Then if a word ends in *-y*, we change the ending to *-ies*. That is, one *penny*, but five *pennies*, unless it is a sum of money and then we say 5 *pence*. It's *i before e except after c except when it doesn't* all over again, i.e. the logic of English is less than logical.

The Audi Quattro inspiration got me thinking about the use of the number four in English and one particular recent phenomenon, the Chelsea Tractor. These are very big cars that are used by affluent school-run mums for so-called "on-roading" activities such as taking up two spaces in the Waitrose car park. In case you didn't know, these vehicles are capable of mounting a kerb with ease and scattering pedestrians when trying to park on double yellow lines while "I only popped into the futon shop for a moment." They are also called four-by-fours. Often written 4by4, this title has puzzled me for some time. 4by4 means four times four. 4x4 = 16. What has the number sixteen to do with Range Rovers and the like?

Now, what you possibly didn't notice was that I managed to present a chapter about the use of numbers in the English language disguised as something else. If I had headed the chapter somewhat like "A short discourse on the use of numbers in language" you would have acted like a triskaidekaphobe and skipped the whole thing. Teachers up and down the land are familiar with this technique. Think of this scenario. It is Friday afternoon, pouring with rain all day. Students have been confined indoors. The local team are playing against a Premiership side in the FA cup tomorrow. This week's hottest boy band is miming live, in person to a backing tape at a local venue. The windows are steamed up. The atmosphere in the class is so thick that you can touch it. 'Now listen up class,' says the teacher. 'Get your exercise books out. We are going to study grammar'.

The reaction is an initial stunned silence, followed by 'nyugh', 'aargh' and 'ooo-ooh'. Very little that would pass for learning would take place that afternoon. But the teacher is an old hand. She says: 'Right, I realise that your minds are someplace else this afternoon and I only have inert bodies in front of me. So we won't do the lesson on grammar that I had planned for this afternoon. Instead we shall play a game.' The content of the lesson is the same. Just the packaging has been made more appealing by calling it a game. You might regard it as deception. Teachers use it as an everyday classroom technique.

By the way, if you thought that the title of this chapter was a bit contrived what will spelling checkers make of hexakosioihexekontohexaphobia? I was sent this in an e-mail in response to a newspaper interview that I gave. Apparently it is a fear of the number 666, the number of the beast or the figure representing the devil. Will it ever end? If you believe the hexakosioihexekontohexaphobes[1] it will. Just look out for all the sixes.

[1] I have not managed to find a dictionary that contains this word so that I can check it. But it sounds good. So, just like the grammar fascists and their beliefs, why should I let a little thing like the truth get in the way of a good story?

We owe a lot to maths. Consider these expressions that derive from mathematics (well geometry if I may stretch the point) that are everyday sayings: vicious circle, learning curve, the bottom line, point of no return, attention span, square meal, parallel universe, pyramid selling, love triangle. We can also rule things out.

There is a word for a successor to a film, sequel. What happens if two films spawn a third and it isn't meant to be a trilogy. We get a threequel. If a film is set before the first one, then it is a prequel and if it is set in between two films it is an interquel. How many is a billion? If you are American, there is only one answer; 1,000,000,000. This amount used to be known to traditionally-minded British people as a thousand million. But the financial press realised that writing and discussing thousand millions was awkward. Despite a certain lack of logical tidiness (see chapter 16), the American system was seen as more convenient. So, the traditional British billion, that is a million million or 1,000,000,000,000, was quietly abandoned. This sum is what the Americans call a trillion. But very few people, surely, keep to the old numbers. In the white heat of Harold Wilson's government, the British officially went for the American system in reporting statistics in 1967. What the government was doing was abandoning the long scale and an alternative word to thousand million: milliard. The long scale still uses 1 followed by 12 noughts to be a billion and is in use in most European countries. So can we even talk of a British billion anymore? If you are neither British nor American, you can take your pick! (Both systems were invented by the French, but are called 'British' and 'American' for convenience.) Both systems have been used in France at various times in history, but France has now settled with the long scale, in common with most other European countries.

At junior schools all over the country, pupils will be writing stories about monsters, dragons or dinosaurs 'as big as a house'. Why should this be? Well children like writing about monsters, dragons and dinosaurs, but also because the childhood perception of something very big is often to compare it with a house. Most kids of 8, 9 or 10 years old have a shared view of the size of a house, pretty big and, in the case of monsters, dragons and dinosaurs therefore very scary. In 20 years time these kids will become doctors, nurses and therapists and each will have a different perception of a house. The size of things is a very important concept in language. Adults have individual perceptions of size, shape and form. Writers often avoid using figures by making comparisons with everyday objects and concepts.

We might be told that an object weighs as much as a bag of sugar. A standard bag of sugar weighs a kilo – so why not say so? I remember reading that the population of Iceland would only fill Wembley Stadium twice. Wembley could take 100,000 before restrictions reduced the capacity to 92,000 and then further when it was made all-seater. Wembley has now been re-built. Most people have no idea of the capacity of the new Wembley, much less people who have no interest at all in stadiums. Something may be described as being as big as 4 football pitches.

But which pitch? At Moss Rose, the poetically-named home of Macclesfield Town, the pitch measures 100 by 66 yards (!) Carlisle United's pitch at Brunton Park is 117 yards long and 72 yards wide. According the FIFA rules, the area of a football pitch can vary between 4,050 m² and 10,880 m². Even non-mathematicians can see that the largest pitch could have more than twice the area of the smallest. The next time someone boasts to you that their garden is as big as a football pitch, find out if it's a Brunton Park or a Moss Rose. I read about a private yacht (don't you just love that cute spelling?) that is as long as 22 London buses. First let's assume that everyone knows what a London bus looks like. So is the length of the yacht 22 buses placed end-to-end? In that case it is quite long. However, if they are placed side-by-side side the length is only the same as one bus. But then, by convention, the shorter length of the assembled buses is the width, so that the resulting measurement is only the equivalent of about 3 or 4 buses placed end-to-end. Whichever, neither comparison is impressive and certainly wouldn't describe the huge size that the writer meant to convey. But we don't all know what length a London bus is. The red double-decker that most people would recognise as one of the quintessential icons of London, the Routemaster, has all but disappeared. I understand that there are more than a dozen different types of bus operating in the capital, both double- and single-deckers. How long are they? There are now even articulated so-called bendy buses that are around twice as long as the traditional bus. Comparing an area to the size of a country is also quite popular. Small countries tend to get picked on. It is common to discuss areas the size of Wales. How much is a Wales exactly? A Wales is 130 Lichtensteins, but less than one-twentieth of a Sweden. Unless you know what a Wales is, does this make any sense? The oft-quoted statistic that rainforest the size of Belgium is being destroyed every year only has any meaning if you know how large Belgium is and how much rainforest there is in the world. Wouldn't it be better to say that if the current rate of rainforest destruction continues there will be no rainforest at all in 20 years or how many it is.

I have no objection to bags of sugar, Wembley stadiums, or even Waleses[1], just please, journalists and others, who feel the need to make graphic comparisons, give us the figures alongside so we can draw our own mental pictures.

[1] The area of Wales is 20,779 km², a London bendy bus is about 18 metres long and the new Wembley has a capacity of 90,000 and a roof area of 11 acres (I wonder, how many football pitches that is?)

15. Splendid isolation

He who lives in solitude may make his own laws.

Publilius Syrus

The main problem is that we have given English to the world, but the ungrateful people in the four corners of the globe have spat it back in our faces. They have distorted the beautiful sound, destroyed the meaning of words and desecrated our grammar system. Or so the *Ellies* believe. Strictly they should be called the *LEs*, but that doesn't make a very good word. *LE* stands for *Little Englander*. There is a sect of grammar fascism that concerns itself with the supposed superiority of British English. By British, naturally, is meant English. Generations of Scottish children learnt about the history of Scotland and England. English kids, on the other hand, learnt solely *English* history but it was called *British* history. Indeed, if you ask an ellie what he thinks of Scotland, he will probably tell you that he rarely thinks about Scotland at all.

As you might expect, the only acceptable forms of English are ones which the grammar fascists themselves approve. *The Guardian* reported: "The English don't need to define themselves- they just are!"

English is like a sponge, soaking up vocabulary from languages around the world. The British Empire was a great source of new words. India has provided many including *bungalow*, *dinghy*, *chutney*, *pundit* and *pyjamas*. These words may be acceptable for grammar fascists as they all come from the empire. Some loan words originate from contact between the British military and locals. If someone takes a *dekko*, they investigate something. The origin is the Hindi *dekho* meaning *look! Shufti*, also meaning to take a look, is another term brought in by ex-servicemen. This comes from Arabic and means 'have you seen?' A whole book could be dedicated to words from the empire and colonies. It will suffice with just one more example, *shampoo*. Known for over 200 years, the word comes from the Hindi *chāmpo,* the imperative of *chāmpnā,* 'to press or squeeze.' This borrowing is significant as it leads to the next area where English is connected to other languages. English has in turn introduced *shampoo* to many, many other countries. The spelling is often changed to take account of local pronunciation and examples include: *schampoo* (Swedish) *sjampo* (Norwegian) *Szampon* (Polish) *Xampu* (Portuguese).

English is the lingua franca, the lingo of Hollywood, the dominant language on the internet as well as the language of so much popular music irrespective of country of origin. Not surprisingly then, English is now the source for many borrowings into foreign languages. What is interesting is that the form of the word or expression may change when it arrives from English. The French *un shampooing* is a clear example. Russian authorities are concerned about *nyu spik* in journalism and advertisements. Words such as *bizinessmyen, footbalist, sexappealnaya* and *mobilny*, And the French complained about *le weekend!* Other countries must have grammar fascists and nationalists too. If this weren't enough, many languages have 'English words' that mean something quite different from the English words. The Germans use *handy* for a mobile phone. Swedes call a Walkman a *freestyle, a* dinner jacket a *smoking* and a computer projector a *beamer.*

There is a further stage where languages adopt 'English words' that don't exist in English.

The Japanese have coined many such words including salaryman to mean an office worker. The modern interplay of languages due to increased international communication means that words like salaryman do appear in English. One of my dictionaries defines it as a white collar worker.

English adopts linguistic style and trends from other countries. American influence is the greatest of these but is excluded here as Americanisms are singled out in the next chapter. Australia has provided us with short forms of words. *Journo* is not unknown for *journalist* and *uni* is almost the standard term for *university*. The Brits are learning to take a more relaxed view of English and the Aussies must surely shoulder some of the praise for this.

Such is the interplay between Englishes that I wonder if we shouldn't say goodbye to hello.

Hey used to be a way of attracting attention: *Hey you*! Now this greeting from the southern states of the USA as established itself in the UK. Its close relative, *hi* has crept quietly but firmly into British usage. Thanks to *Neighbours* and other soaps from down under, *G'day* isn't entirely unknown. Holidays in Spain have added *hola!* It may not be mainstream but yo! is the alternative favoured by some young people. We should also include *wassup?* the fad greeting from Budweiser beer advertisements. I have no idea where it originates but the standard greeting of supermarket checkout staff is *hiya*. Anyway, the traditional British greeting has changed its meaning. Hello now means 'you can't be serious?' Hello?

Should English words from foreign languages retain the accents from the original language? Is it café or cafe? In 2003, *The Observer* revised its style guide. The new guide suggested that foreign words that have become an integral part of the English language such as *cliche*, *detente* and *debacle* should drop the accent. My computer spell checker, however, automatically corrected the first two words to cliché and détente, but not debacle. The Microsoft programmer obviously doesn't read *The Observer*. The style guide went on to say though that words such as *resumé* and *exposé* should keep the accents to avoid confusion with English words spelled the same way but without accents. English doesn't have accents on letters, so this seems very sound advice. What would a grammar fascist make of it though? The purist view might be to retain accents (one supposes indefinitely). The ellie perspective would most likely be that 'British is best' holds sway and all accents should be prevented from polluting the most beautiful language on earth.

Other Englishes now have lives of their own. Indian English is a good example. In Bollywood films in India *item songs* are musical numbers often with dance sequences that have no place in the storyline. The purpose is simply to feature an *item girl*, who would be one of the main attractions for seeing the film. *Singlish* is another strand of English although it is not easily recognised as the English we know. The colonial English of Singapore is mixed with Hokkien Chinese and bits of Malay thrown in for good measure. *Seth Effrican* is another regional variation.

In conclusion, what do the grammar fascists make of all this internationalisation in English? Perhaps geography will give us a clue. Many people speak of Britain <u>and</u> Europe as if the British Isles were in no way connected to our continental neighbours. 30+ years of membership of the European Union have done little to change the way many people betray their feelings linguistically. Europe seems to be the political equivalent of the grockle.

16. Two nations ~~united~~ divided by a common language

An Englishman is a person who does things because they have been done before. An American is a person who does things because they haven't been done before.

Mark Twain

There are people in both in Britain, and around the world, that have some kind of objection to American English. Some of this is just plain prejudice; irrational beliefs formed by some dislike of everything American. British English was spread around the world and reigned supreme when Britain was Great. Nowadays, it is American English that has the upper hand, due to the internet, popular music, film ad TV culture. American is seen as young, dynamic and forward looking, British as stuffy and conservative. Perhaps this has generated a sense of inadequacy. The ellies who we met in the last chapter possibly suffer from an inferiority complex. So there is a kind of grammar fascism that brands American English as second-rate. If there were a political party called Let's Knock All Things American I'm sure that it would get a few votes. I have examples from discussion boards that have nothing to do with language under headings such as "Worst 10 Americanisms."

Some even try to justify classifying American English as second-rate with pseudo-intellectual arguments. The gist of what they are saying is that American English is the wayward child of the mother tongue who adopted bad ways during a lengthy period of absence from home. British English is authentic, American is synthetic. British is polite and humble; the US version is rude and brash. In Britain the sound of the language is beautiful and flowing; in the United States it is a lazy drawl. The Americans have ruined the spelling system, lost where to put commas, forgotten the correct use of prepositions and use words that shouldn't really exist. In short, American English is illogical and has no sense of history. Hopefully, I shall show all these arguments to be false. American English is equal to any other variety and just as valid.

When it comes to Americanisms, grammar fascists really get their knickers in a twist, well their pants twisted. They get so upset when Americans call trousers *pants*. *Pants* are what you wear under your trousers. Or are they? The American usage of pants derives from the French, *pantalon*. The British use of pants is actually a shortened form of underpants, as they were called pantaloons in Britain too. Here, surely the Americans are closest to the original meaning. For those that say that Americans lack history, I say only two words, *real estate*. This comes from when William I asserted his jurisdiction over all land disputes. Ownership squabbles were royal actions in the kings court. As Norman French was the language of the law, *real* was used for *royal* hence real estate. America with its president uses the term, Britain with its monarch no longer does. While we in Britain dropped certain words after the independence of the United States, the Americans retained them. In Britain we lost *fall* for *autumn* and *mad* in the sense of *angry*. Two typical American words have long pedigrees. *Janitor* (widely used in Scotland) comes from Latin and *teller* (someone who works as a cashier in a bank and also the standard term in Scotland) is from an Old English verb meaning to count.

The Ellies, no doubt, object to opening of the linguistic floodgates causing British English to be awash with American words and phrases. The problem is that we have too many police shows on TV. Aren't you getting fed up with hearing about *homicide*? Why can't they use the good old English; *murder*? John Milton used *homicide* more than 100 years before the USA came into existence and about 3 centuries before American cop series. Such a large number of so-called American isms are good and very old English words that went out of fashion in Britain, but continued to be used in the USA. The US still has *sheriffs* as part of law-enforcement. In Britain where there is a sheriff, the office is largely ceremonial. Go to the USA and you will see *yield* written on signs and painted on the tarmac at road junctions. This good old English word, that may conjure up images of knights in shining armour battling to the death or until one gives up, is in common use in the USA. In Britain we have signs that say "GIVE WAY".

Some people can get annoyed by the fact that some Americanisms are difficult to understand. I know few people who have truly understood the meaning of the term *rain check*. The term originated at baseball games in America, the ticket is often in three parts. You surrender one part on entry to the stadium. You keep the ticket and a rain check which you can use to get a ticket for another game or a refund if rain stops play before the fifth innings has been completed. I discovered this when watching the Chicago Cubs during an afternoon in late June when lightning was striking buildings all around Wrigley Field. The players rushed through the first 5 innings in about 45 minutes. The following 4 innings took almost 2 hours. I suppose they wanted to get to the point where they wouldn't have to refund any money before the heavens opened. Mind you. they needn't have bothered, because so few people were watching the game as they were preoccupied with pretzels and popcorn and beer. The term rain check is in general language use. *To take a raincheck* is a polite way to turn down an invitation while implying that another occasion would be acceptable. It is the implication that most non-Americans miss, although I know from those wonderful Flying Doctors, that the Australians understand the term fully.

Sticking with the sporting theme, there are those who might admonish Americans because of their vulgar athletic pursuits. Upstart games like baseball for example. Published in 1818, *Northanger Abbey* by Jane Austen has Catherine Morland prefer "cricket, base ball, riding on horseback and running about the country at the age of 14 to books." This was long before the Americans stopped playing cricket and took up baseball (if it is indeed the same game). I think it should also be pointed out that the first international cricket match had nothing at all to do with England or indeed anywhere else in the Empire. It was played in front of 10,000 spectators at Bloomingdale Park in New York in 1844. The two teams were the United States and Canada. In fact this could well be the oldest international sporting event in the modern world. Who ever accused the Americans of lacking tradition?

A dyed-in the wool ellie, (shame it isn't died in the wool) will chastise the colonials for not adding the word *American* before their kind of football. They should follow our example. Brits always, without exception, put *Association* and *Rugby* before the f-word, to indicate the version of the game. While slipping in the odd reminder that baseball is a British invention, ellies will ridicule the idea that culmination of the season is called the World Series. "World Series. World Series!" (*rising volume and heightened tone of indignation*). How can you call a competition the World Series if only teams from one country are allowed to play? What's that? There are Canadian teams too? I see. That's the trick, is it? Invite a team or two from Canada to make it seem international. Typical American view of things. They think North America is the world. Ignore Canada except when they need it to legitimise their global perspective. And 80% of Americans have never been abroad..." ('continue until closing time'). What is forgotten here, or to be more accurate, not learnt in the first place, is where the *World* of *World Series* comes from. The competition was started as a way of boosting newspaper circulation. The idea was to start a baseball championship. This would extend the season and sell more copies. The competition between the two top teams was named after the newspaper; *The New York World*. So, baseball simply has the equivalent of the Barclays Premiership. However, as with so many other things, the American thought of sponsorship well before the British. When the truth is known, the *Americaphobes* have one less 'fact' with which to tease the Yankees and the Red Sox. But why have the truth when we can make something up and isn't it irritating how they insist on spelling the word *socks*?

So many Britishisms originate in the USA anyway and we don't even notice or know when an Americanism has come into our language. This is the famous British stiff upper lip I suppose. Or is it? The earliest known example of the phrase comes from the Massachusetts Spy in 1815: "I kept a stiff upper lip, and bought license to sell my goods." It turns up throughout the 1800s in American literature. Mark Twain used it. It wasn't until towards the end of the century that it began to appear on this side of the Atlantic and with the word British attached. I understand that 80% of all neologisms in British English originate in the United States. That's 4 new words out of every 5. The language would grind to a halt if it wasn't for the ex-colonies!

The grammar fascists trying to stem the tide of Americanisms especially dislike the fact that in the USA people often use words for the *toilet* or *lavatory* such as *bathroom* or *restroom*. Remember Dr Law from chapter 1? He wrote in his letter: "After visiting the toilet I usually wash my hands in the lavatory itself …a lavatory is a wash-hand basin not a water closet..." Well, unbeknowingly perhaps, he was siding with the Americans. The Yanks <u>have</u> got it right. A bathroom is a kind of washing place or lavatory. Yah boo, sucks to you grammar fascists! Although, there is another state-side toilet euphemism, much derided from Britain, that I am prepared to take a dig at. On my first visit to the United States, I was in an up-market burger joint (up market in this case means they had tablecloths) and hungry enough to eat almost anything. I got up from the table and looked around for the restroom as I wished to wash my hands before "dining" in a cutleryless sort of way. Looking lost, I was asked by a member of staff:

"Are you looking for the restroom?"
"Indeed I am. Maybe there are some pillows and a blanket as I could do with a little lie down."
"Sorry, sir?"
"You said you had a restroom and I thought... Oh never mind, it's that way, is it?"

We should do like the Canadians and call it a washroom. Because not only should we wash our hands after going to the toilet but we can also find agreement with the good doctor's definition of lavatory!

There are plenty of people who complain about the Americanisation of British English. There is certainly plenty of evidence. Small milk cartons in Tescos, Britain's biggest retailer, are marked TO GO! The following sign in another leading supermarket, Morrisons, "Cheese packed to go at no extra cost." Why is the American *to go* preferred to the British *takeaway*? It isn't. Takeaway is not appropriate in this context. This is complementary meaning rather than a replacement.

In the Norwich branch of the travel agent Thomas Cook there was a hand-written sign that said "500 Euro bills, special rate 1.405." A bill is a form of invoice stating how much you have to pay for say electricity, gas or the telephone. British people have *notes* in their wallets and purses irrespective of the country of origin (with respect, naturally, to the mighty Yankee dollar).

There is a rapid response team employed by Norwich City Council. When someone calls the office to complain about litter in the streets, their task is to immediately go clear it up. On the side of the vehicles is the legend SWAT. This is the SWAT team. But has anyone considered what the acronym SWAT means? Borrowed from American police jargon (no doubt via endless police series on TV), SWAT means Strategic Weapons Assault Team. In LA the SWAT team dressed in flak jackets and carrying automatic weapons would race to the scene of a bank robbery. In Norwich they hurry as fast as a diesel-powered Ford Transit will allow and get out their brushes and shovels! But it is neither the Americans nor their language that is at fault here. It is whoever decided that SWAT was appropriate to street cleaning. One might complain that it is second-rate use of language and then again because second-rate itself is an Americanism. However, despite a popular belief about its stateside origins, the term comes from the Royal Navy. Old wooden warships were given a rating according to the number of guns. First rate was over 100 guns, second rate 90 to 100 and so on. So some Americanisms are actually as British as fish and chips.

A British newspaper had an article concerning "Britain's 10 longest serving PMs (longest single term of office)." Quick off the mark, the letters flooded in about this howler. British prime ministers don't have terms of office. Apart from the maximum of 5 years, the tenure of office is not fixed. Unlike the President of the United States, the British prime minister can call an election at any time. Does it matter? My local MP, Charles Clarke, has also referred to the government's *current term of office*. I am told he has used this phrase a number of times. Way to go, Charles! This is a good term (sorry about the cheap pun, it was irresistible). Term has become adapted to the British context. We all know the British system is different to the American. In a similar vein, there is another phrase adopted from the USA in the political arena that gets some people hot under the collar. Politicians don't run for office, they stand for election, the hard-liners cry in anguish. Why not let them do both? Surely English is enriched by having more than one way to express the same thing.

There was a complaint in *The Guardian* about Americanisms that picked upon a BBC correspondent who "managed to use what may be the ugliest word ever invented, 'gotten', instead of 'got.'" *Gotten* has been around since the 14th century. It dropped out of use in Britain more than 100 years ago. It's still used in America, but it is far from correct to call it an Americanism. Nothing's rotten about gotten just because Brits have forgotten it.

In an article discussing the possibility of an incident similar to the Madrid train bombing, *The Observer* ran the headline: "Anti-terror marshals to ride trains. " Marshalls? This conjures up images of Wyatt Earp and the Gunfight at the OK Corral. We have police and detectives, but no marshals. They are American. Although we might take a train ride, we don't ride trains in Britain, we travel on them. The verb is somewhat different from the noun.[1] But again, why not?. It is a new concept for Britain to have security forces on public transport, a name is required and the Americans have a perfectly good one that we can borrow. Thank you.

Another headline that shows the extent of Americanisation ran: "Euro vote too close to call with Sweden in mourning." Calling comes from baseball, a game hardly played in Britain apart from on US Air Force bases in Suffolk and Lincolnshire. There are quite a number of baseball analogies: *ball park figure*, *out of left field*, *big-hitter* and the so-called *three strikes law*. A spokesman for the London Stock Exchange told BBC television: "Companies are stepping up to the plate and investing £100 million." Does it matter that we neither play nor understand the game? Baseball terms enliven British English.

Hopefully, I have dismissed some of the illogicalities about American English and disarmed the ellies of a few prejudices. After the title page, many books have the line: "For copyright reasons,

[1]Did you spot the pedant's way?

this edition is not for sale in the USA." Some ellies might wish to add: "...as they wouldn't understand it." I have very few issues with American English. However, there are American grammar fascists too. Not so very long ago, I was giving a course for teachers in Stockholm on, appropriately enough, American English. I give lectures to teachers from state schools as I am ideologically opposed to private education unless they pay me well enough.

I received a phone call from a chap asking if there were any places left. "Yes," I said, "there are three places left." When I enquired after his place of work, he said that he was not employed by a school, but was freelance. I wondered why he, now obvious by his accent, an American, wanted to attend my course. He couldn't give me an answer (or how he would pay for the course). So I said that I was sorry but he couldn't attend. He questioned my authority to exclude him. I presented him with two reasons why I didn't want him to attend the course. The ensuing discussion was interrupted.

American: No, it's *eether*
Me: Sorry?
American: You mispronounced the word"
Me: (long dumbfounded silence)
American: It's *eether*.
Me: (recovering) You are American? Am I right?
American: Yes.
Me: And, in the USA you exclusively pronounce the word *eether*?
American: Yes.

155

Me: I'm from England. You may have
           guessed. We have two pronunciations;
           eether and *eyether*. It just so happens
           that I come from a part of the country
           where we usually say eyether. We Brits
           can choose. Oh sorry, I must have
           miscounted, the course is indeed full.
           Goodbye.

What I should have said was: "I don't think that
you should attend my course because there is
nothing that I could possibly teach you. You Sir, are
both arrogant and a bigot. Furthermore, you are
the first and only rude American that I have
encountered." I am sorry to say that this number
has now grown to two. But this is still a very good
percentage. Do you want to know about the other
one? Sorry, he was so obnoxious and so ill-informed
about British English I wouldn't waste a line of
print on him, although I can offer him a few words
of advice. You won't get a job at proper university
until you drop your prejudice about British English
that makes you as bad as all the anti-Americans.
Please, do something about your linguistic
inferiority complex oh, and stop reminding
everyone every 5 minutes that you are a doctor!

I must admit to once having a sense of unease
about some American universities. How do we
know that an academic institution is real? I used to
be rather suspicious concerning higher education in
the USA. In Britain we are used to a university
being of a place, even if it is Luton. In America,
colleges, as they also like to call them, are often
named after a benefactor. I must have received

thousands of spam e-mails offering me all kinds of university degrees. Why did I waste all those years studying, when $399 and an essay that is a summary of my life so far would achieve the same result? When asked about my qualifications I used to say that I've got a PhD from the Bob Jones University of Life. Then, whilst passing through Greenville in South Carolina, I discovered that there is indeed a *Bob Jones University*. It is possible to check if a college is more than an e-mail address and a bank account to pay into. If it has a campus and a football team then it is most likely legitimate. Bob Jones removed my misconception about American universities.

Please can we do away with the stereotypes in American television and films? British people do not all have bad teeth. There are more types of British English than the untutored Eliza Doolittle or the disorientated Hugh Grant. Also why are Britons so often the baddies and why does Mel Gibson hate us so much? Was he bullied by a Pom back in Australia as a child? Finally, when a successful British sitcom is remade for American audiences, why do they first take out the *sit* and then the *com*.

The odd thing is that British and American can hardly be regarded as two separate languages. They are very similar. In September 2000, I was driving in southern Sweden while trying to listen to Radio 4 on long wave. The reception was poor. But I could make out the voice of David Crystal, probably the greatest living expert on English this side of the Atlantic. In a discussion, he said that, apart from pronunciation, the differences between British and

American English are insignificant. This haunted me for some time, until I finally got round to testing his bold assertion. I selected an American book at random and let it fall open. The book is *Fast Food Nation*, the page is 158. I counted the words on the page to answer the question: 'How often do differences occur between American and British English?'

Looking for Americanisms of all kinds, I found:

Total number of words	410
American words	1
Missing hyphens	1
Compounded words	3
Spelling	2
Missing prepositions	1
Total Americanisms	8

So, 8 Americanisms out of 410 words. That is 2% or 2 words in every 100. Turn that figure around and we see that 98% is the same in both British and American English. So why do grammar fascists get so uptight about the differences between the two dialects of the same language?

The last word should come from someone who knows both Britain and America very well. For 58 years, until just before his death in February 2004, Alistair Cook broadcast a weekly *Letter from America*. He often commented on the English used in the United States. His message was to help us Brits understand America and the Americans. Cook was once asked if he was British or American. He replied: "Can't I be both?"

17. People Like Us

No one can make you feel inferior without your consent.

Eleanor Roosevelt

People Like Us does not mean that people like us. This has nothing to do with being liked or otherwise. People Like Us is the term that People Like Us use to show who belongs to a closed group of similar or like-minded people. Therefore, as most of us aren't People Like Us, we should really say People Like Them. The problem is that we don't know who they are. The only way that anyone knows who belongs to People Like Us is when someone says 'they aren't People Like Us.' It is only by being excluded from the group that you will know that you are not People Like Us. So, how do the People Like Us know that they are People like Us? Take it from me, they just know. Grammar fascists are People Like Us. This chapter is about the grammar fascists themselves. They would not say 'people like us.' They know that when it comes to a scale of likedness, grammar fascists come right at the very bottom. This does not deter them. For, being People Like Us, they believe themselves to be superior to just about anyone else. Which explains why they think that people like them, but in fact no-one likes people Like Us except other People Like Us.

Who writes grammar books anyway? In the main, a certain type of person, with a given level of education, a social standing who dare I say it is probably a ...grammar fascist! Actually that isn't true. There are some good grammars that have been written by people who are anything but pedants. But the relationship between a certain type of person and sticklerism is quite likely. Here is one piece of evidence.

Those of us who have no problems with the spelling of our own language are being asked to unlearn orthographical skills in favour of the demands of the orthographically challenged. How about them getting their heads down and coming up to our level - or is having standards now too deeply unfashionable for discussion?
Tom Anderson
Greater Manchester

Kindly note: "coming up to our level." Everyone else is therefore below. Is Mr Anderson implying that anyone who does not match his lofty heights of eloquence is lazy and not worthy? This is the peacock-like air of superiority that People Like Us like to display. Not only do they have to feel superior, they have to let the great unwashed know that they excel in language just in case we hadn't noticed.

People Like Us believe that they speak standard English and everyone else is a deviant. You might say that standard English is 'standard white English,' or 'standard white male English,' or 'standard white male middle-class English.' This is a relationship less about language norms, but more about whiteness, sex and class. Importantly it is about power. Political and financial power happens to be in the hands of white, middle class males. So what is standard English I wonder?

Not that long ago, while travelling by train, I sat opposite a middle-aged man reading a dictionary. Yes, he was reading a dictionary, just as you or I might read a novel. He had a book mark and opened the book somewhere early in the Gs. He read all the way from Waterloo to Bournemouth. Reading the headline words upside down, I could see that he read from gerrymander to godforsaken[1], while the train rattled on. I watched the quivers of delight as he came across words that he obviously loved and little winces at definitions that were in some way unsatisfactory. He even laughed out loud as the train approached Winchester. I'm sure that this man had a genuine love for words. But while some people read books on trains because there is no-one to talk to, I do wonder if grammar fascists read books on trains because of the risk that someone <u>will</u> talk to them.

The train ride set me thinking, what do Grammar fascists do when not writing letters to newspapers? I suspect that grammar fascists play word games. Not for the enjoyment of playing, but to crush the opposition or show how clever they are. While stranded in a hut on a mountainside on a

[1]I wonder if there is some grammar fascist who, armed with the information about the headline words, knows which dictionary the man was reading from or is now so smitten with curiosity that he is determined to find out?

Pacific island during a tropical rainstorm, would you believe that in a small rucksack of travel items someone had a Scrabble set. Now, I have never read the rules of Scrabble in their entirety. For me, the rules have always been if everyone else accepted a word, it is allowable. If not, tough luck. Try again. For this one particular grammar fascist, only the official Scrabble dictionary was acceptable as arbiter of acceptable words. Arrange your letters to make bize or oxim and you are sure to get rid of one of those awkward but high-scoring letters[2]. I got fed up with hearing that her weird words were totally acceptable because they are in the dictionary. So, I started to make up my own words. "Qoph," I explained, "is a letter in the Arabic alphabet, while lin is Gaelic for flax - as in linseed oil or linen." Not only could I invent definitions, but I could appeal to a higher authority, *The Oxford English Dictionary*. If I had to accept her rulings from a dictionary that I couldn't consult, then 1000 metres up a mountain, she had to accept mine. As luck would have it, they are both real words. Qoph is actually a letter in the Hebrew alphabet. Lin is the Swedish for flax, but I knew I couldn't get away with that. Also, it is most probably related to the words I used in my definition (look it up!), but making it Gaelic made it credible given the history of linen production in Ulster. I later found out that lin is the chief alkaloid of the betel nut. The moral of this story is simple. When a grammar fascist tries to baffle you by appealing to invisible

[2]These two words are included in the online Scrabble dictionary!

references, just go higher and bluff, bluff and bluff again. The language is so vast you might just be right.

I think that grammar fascists might also try to invent pangrams. For non-grammar fascists a *pangram* is a sentence that contains all 26 letters of the alphabet. *The quick brown fox jumps over the lazy dog* is probably the most famous example. This sentence has 34 letters. The challenge is to find one which contains all 26 letters only once. The nearest I have heard of uses just the letters *i* and *u* twice: *Brick quiz whangs jumpy veldt fox*. Before you ask; no, I don't know what whanging is and I have no burning desire to find out, although I can make an educated guess. Grammar fascists will either know or look it up. Normal folks can cope with not knowing the precise meaning of every word they encounter. Please accept my apologies if you do know or have already looked it up. A *lipogram* is another kind of letter exercise that might prevent a mind from being empty. Lipograms are compositions that omit a certain letter. Perhaps the most difficult form of lipogram omits the letter *e* as it occurs most often in English. Ernest Vincent Wright wrote a novel called *Gadsby*. He managed 50,000 words without a single *e*. Georges Perec's work, *La Disparition*, had 300 pages. It was translated into e-less English by Gilbert Adair in 1995 as *A Void*.

Crosswords, naturally, are in grammar fascist territory. This is especially so as there are a number of conventions that apply. If you learn the conventions then you can solve any cryptic crossword. Crossword clues can be anagrams.

Making anagrams can be fun. Rearranging letters in a name or phrase to make another name or phrase could be another activity for the linguistically determined. Here are two anagrams of grammar fascists:

GRAMMAR FACTS IS
SARCASM FAT GRIM

I like the grim sarcasm of the second anagram. The anagramist grammar fascists will enjoy working on my name as it contains the possibility to make words such as alas, hate and satanic.

There are some gaps in the English language. One gap encourages grammar fascists to be sexist. English has no singular gender-neutral pronoun that we can use when we don't know if someone is male or female. There is *it*. However, we can only use *it* for objects or animals. The issue today is one of fairness and not to make any assumptions about the gender of a person. There are three possibilities:

First, consider this sentence: *A firefighter must adhere to the following procedure before he/she enters a burning building.* Correct, but it doesn't let the text flow and is somewhat cumbersome, especially if it has to be repeated over and over again.

Second, we can fall back on something that increasing Americans seem to favour: WWJD? What Would Jane (Austen) Do? In *Pride and Prejudice*, the narrator explains about Mr

Wickham: "Every body declared that he was the wickedest young man in the world; and every body began to find out that they had always distrusted the appearance of his goodness." Grammar fascists can't accept this as *they* is plural and doesn't agree with the singular *every body*.

Third, we have the traditional view. *In the olden days when someone wrote seditiously, he would be punished by transportation to Van Dieman's land.* Older style manuals would support using the male personage here. Grammar fascists support this sentence in its entirety as it is the only one that is grammatically correct for them. This is how grammar fascists, intentionally or otherwise, expose themselves as sexist.

There are other possibilities. One is to write only *she* and *her*. But I think this equally as unacceptable as using *him or his*. Another is to alternate between male and female within the text. Wearisome to the reader though. Of course there are people who would re-write the sentence to completely remove the issue. For example: *they* could be replaced by another *every body* in the Jane Austen example. Although this wouldn't look good as there would be three instances of *every body* in the same sentence. Sometimes completely re-writing is tricky and why, indeed should anyone bother. So, failing the possibility that someone invents a new pronoun to cover this eventuality and not wanting to rewriting the sentence, then I'm a supporter of St Jane. Thackeray wrote in *Vanity Fair* "A person can't help their birth." As well as providing an example of non-sexist language, perhaps this statement gives us a clue about People Like Us.

PLUs are not PC. An import from the States, politically correct language is all about using terms that don't offend people. For example, instead of using terms like *crippled* or *handicapped*, we might use *disabled* or even *physically challenged*. The aim is to emphasise the positive aspects of people who are not fully able-bodied, reflecting the can-do attitude of most disabled people. If you were asked to clothe yourself using only one foot do you think that you could do it?

In 2004, that year's leader of the Conservative Party, Michael Howard, proclaimed: "I will end the insanity of political correctness." But this prime minister-in-waiting wasn't talking about political correctness at all. Amongst other things, his speech was about the right of people to defend themselves in their own homes. He wasn't talking about the unofficial offence of 'driving while black.' Sadly, that put Mr H firmly in the sphere of the grammar fascists as what he actually meant was ideas that he didn't agree with. Grammar fascists don't have to be consistent. They can criticise one thing, but leave another well alone. The rationale is simple. Apart from anything else, they answer only to themselves. The opinions of you or me or any of the 400 million other native speakers of English are quite simply not valid. We are not qualified as we are not People Like Us.

PLUs don't live in the real world. They are as in touch as the Duke of Devonshire in the infamous napkin incident. A butler informed the Duke that the middle classes had napkin rings to hold their napkins in between courses. He is reputed to have remarked: "I never knew such poverty existed." He couldn't imagine using the same napkin throughout the meal. This might well be a Marie Antoinette 'let them eat cake' kind of story. Either it is a fabrication or grossly exaggerated. But I tell it because I wonder why grammar fascists behave in the ways that they do. Do they feel threatened? Like wounded, cornered animals they prepare for one last desperate attempt to attack. Society is changing and their natural habitats are being destroyed. *The Times* is now the same size as *The Sun*. ITV make programmes as entertaining and informative as the BBC (or is it that standards at the BBC have declined). No-one addresses me as 'Sir' these days. You can't get kippers like you used to. The paperboy saunters round long after sunrise with a hoodie top pulled up so that you can't make out his face. He can't be bothered to push the paper all the way in so that half gets wet and is unreadable. The post only comes once a day. Are the grammar fascists as PLUs an endangered species? Are we seeing the death-throws, the final convulsions of the reflexes, before the final curtain comes down?

18. Takes one to know one

It's a strange world of language in which skating on thin ice can get you into hot water.

Franklin P. Jones

As the title of the book may suggest and the previous 165 pages have hinted, not only do I like understatement, but I am tolerant with ways to communicate in English. I believe it our duty to vary our vocabulary and expressions, even to the point of taking liberties with the language. But, stretching only as far as communication is maintained and not going past it. Everyone draws the line somewhere as to what is acceptable. Naturally, context is a very important factor. Abstract poetry has no rules and it would be true to say that anything goes. . At the other end of the scale, legal documents are governed by convention and there is little room for experimentation. I believe that wherever possible we should seek out opportunities to break conformity in language and demonstrate individuality. In complaining about grammar fascists, I have painted a picture of grumpy old men finding faults in the English of others. If I have exposed some of the common language grievances as misguided, I need to give the whingers and whiners something legitimate to moan about. There are a number of areas where the use of English could or perhaps should give grammar fascists something to complain about. Most of these gripes are misdemeanours rather than felonies and this section outlines some legitimate causes to which the pedants can direct their energies.

The language used by call centres is not just annoying, it is insincere and dishonest. When I hear the message: "Thank you for waiting, an operator will be with you momentarily," I know that it is a lie. A moment is how long? Not the 30 minutes it takes to speak to a human being because your gas and electricity is now supplied by British Gas, when you didn't ask for it. I also know that it is a lie when a recorded message repeats from a loop that: "Your call is important to us, please hold." I regard, 'we value your call' as a statement of no worth whatsoever. If our calls were truly valued, then we wouldn't have to "listen carefully" to the following options" before finding that no combination of pressing figures, stars and hashes will get us anywhere more than back to the main menu (and why do they call it a menu anyway). Of course, the companies providing the service (a misnomer if ever there was one) do value the call as they are charging us the national rate (this is call centre speak for 'Ha, ha, we actually earn money all the time we keep you on hold).

Equally irritating is when someone asks if I can confirm my address. When this happened recently, I waited for the lady to say my address, so that I could confirm it. After a pause, she repeated the question. I said that I could indeed and waited once more. Of course what she wanted, was for me to tell her my address. Why didn't she ask me for my address in the first place, instead of what was on her script? When someone says: "I empathise with you, Mr. Waters." They are actually saying;: 'I couldn't care less. All I want you to think is that something will be done, but my only intention is to get rid of you as soon as possible.'

Attention should be given to those who want to give up addictive substances such as profanities. Unless the referee has denied us a clear penalty there is no need ever to swear. However, if you can't avoid it consider one of the substitutes. There are plenty of euphemisms that can be used instead. The f-word has been with us since the 15th century, so we have had over 500 years to think up replacements. Although we haven't been incredibly inventive, there are several options: *flipping*, *furkin* or *effing* from British English. The Irish use *feckin'* and the Americans have *freakin'*. Then of course, there are words like *chuffin'* that are especially useful when there are children present as it doesn't even sound like the word it replaces. Sometimes a warning is given at the start of a TV programme such as: "This programme contains strong language." After hearing the f-word used repeatedly, I would say that using swear words only weakens it.

Alistair Cooke's Christmas 1967 *Letter from America* noted that four-letter words are being used so much that there won't be any left for special occasions.

Watching TV, I am still amazed how quickly the BBC, ITN and Sky can get a television crew out to a newsworthy event. What doesn't surprise me is that eyewitnesses, relatives and anyone remotely connected with the happening will be asked how they feel. The purpose is to show how upset they are at the happening. This is intrusive. How would you like to be asked how you feel having been pulled from a train wreck? Also it can be argued that how you feel is not connected to your feelings (thoughts) but your physical condition. The standard answer from these poor people in shock is all too often: "I'm devastated," which means I was very upset. I don't object to the hyperbole. I don't care to consider any possible etymological fallacy about the true meaning of devastated. What I complain about is the ubiquity of this statement. It is almost as if, prior to any interview with a distraught person, they have been reminded to look tearfully into the camera and utter exactly that short phrase. If I hear one more person say: "I'm devastated" I will be forced to write a letter. Not to newspaper, but to the TV news desks. I could to ask them each to consult a thesaurus and run a short course for their reporters. The on-the-spot team can then brief interviewees in optional phrases to use instead of the one that means 'laid to waste, rendered desolate.'

Murdering the language is a result of thoughtlessness in journalism. This letter appeared in *The Independent:*

Sir: "Executed in coldblood, aged 7" screams your headline. No, "executed" means "put to death by law." The word you want is "murdered." By misusing "execute" you lose a valuable distinction and thus contribute to the impoverishment of the English language.

JJ Grimond
London W11

I can't say that I concur that the language has been impoverished. However, I certainly agree that murder is the only appropriate word. Gangland execution is a misnomer, so is *'honour killing.'* First it is murder and second, there is no honour in murdering someone, let alone someone in your own family who has broken some outdated code of behaviour that usually concerns the suppression of women. Honour is a positive word and should not be used as it removes some of the gravity of the word murder. And, while we are on the subject, there is another term that I would like to kick into touch, *female circumcision*. This disgusting physical attack on young women should be given a proper description such as *female genital mutilation* or simply *causing grievous bodily harm*. The practice should be made a crime the whole world over, its perpetrators punished so severely that it disappears. In a similar vein, when generals talk about *collateral damage* we can be sure that they mean the *deaths of innocent civilians*. When *death* is mentioned in war, the next thought is to wonder who did the killing. By allowing the use of neutral terms such as *damage* we tend not to think of human lives being lost and therefore do not apportion blame. Part of any conflict, especially in the current media age, is to win the propaganda battle. Orwell's *doublethink* and *newspeak* come to mind. *Collateral damage* is a weapon of mass distraction.

John Simpson, the veteran TV reporter, was hit by 'friendly fire' while reporting on the Iraq war. Friendly fire can be accidental when the target is missed and someone on one's own side is hit. Friendly fire can also be deliberate when the 'enemy' is incorrectly identified and one's own side becomes the target. What must John Simpson and anyone else shot in this way think about using *friendly*?

Hyperbole can be fun. However, thoughtless use of superlatives makes it difficult to find good descriptions of truly momentous events. After a rather exciting third test match between England and Australia, *The Independent* splashed a banner across its front page "THE ULTIMATE TEST." I am a recent convert to watching cricket, so recent that it was only the rather exciting second test that awakened my interest. How sad then that the ultimate test has taken place and I will be unable to watch anymore. But of course, ultimate did not mean last as there indeed followed a fourth and fifth test. Ultimate meant the absolute peak. I didn't watch the fourth and fifth tests because cricket had reached its peak and therefore could only go downhill in quality.

There was a storm while I was in Australia last. The attempt at hyperbole from the reporter sent to the scene was at first really up front: "What strikes me is the utter devastation." But when the camera panned round and his words began to sound a little hollow, he added: "Some trees have been uprooted and some houses destroyed."

The newspaper to which I subscribe had an article in its travel section called "The Complete

Guide to Dorset." The article began: "In many respects, Dorset has it all." Well, it either has it all so that "In many respects" is redundant, or if the "many respects" is correct then Dorset doesn't have it ALL. Fortunately, having been born and bred in Dorset, I do not need the "Complete Guide" as I know of some nice places from local knowledge. I also have no desire to dilute my summer with the hundreds of thousands of grockles that fill up the beach car parks and lengthen the queues outside the ice cream shops. Of course, there are places to go which tourists rarely find. They are directed to spots by the "Complete Guide." This leaves the rest of the county relatively holidaymakerless. You have probably guessed that the "Complete Guide" is anything but comprehensive. But at least the guide did not make the common blunder of revealing any undiscovered places. Off-the-beaten-track, hard-to-find, remote, isolated and deserted are all fine. Undiscovered these days might only apply to remote areas of the Antarctic.

The Guardian ran the headline:

**'UK's hottest
day ever'
warning**

Ignoring the fact that the article didn't back up the direct quote indicated in the headline, I want to complain about the overuse of the word *ever*. To me, the word means without beginning and without end, a bit like *always*. The first definition in the *Collins Dictionary* reads *at any time*. You can qualify *ever* e .g. *ever since* (from a point in time onwards), *forever* or *ever after* (for all the future) and *hardly ever* (almost never). The word in question can also be used to reinforce an expression e.g. *I will never ever set foot in that house again, who ever told you that?* and *that café is ever so nice.* But, on its own, *ever* has this forwards and backwards meaning. So that the headline implies that the 18th July will the hottest day recorded in the UK and that there will be no hotter day. Is *The Guardian* launching a new service where they predict the future or does the environmental correspondent have some information that from the date of the article onwards, it will never be as hot again. Surely *'UK's hottest day' warning* would be sufficient.

"Smoke blows over half the country," was a headline in *The Daily Express*. The accompanying article stated that winds had carried the smoke as far west as Andover and east to the Thames estuary - more than 80 miles. Perhaps, what they should have written was 'smoke blows over London and the *Daily Express* offices.' The accompanying satellite photo didn't even <u>show</u> half the country anyway. Much to the probable delight of any home-counties-based grammar fascists reading the paper that day, the photograph did not even show the country as far north as Manchester. Luckily, one sense of hyperbole is that it shouldn't be taken literally. Perhaps it is the responsibility of readers and listeners not to be taken in by outrageous statements, just as much as it is the duty of the speaker or writer not to make them.

Speculative language is another area of English that could be tidied up. The classic example is when the back pages of newspapers, local or national, devoid of any factual storyline, indulge in speculation such as 'Smith poised to sign for Rovers.' This has led to endless speculation about the outcome of events (often sporting) over which the commentators can exercise no control or have no influence. As a football supporter, I enjoy 90 minutes of entertainment, but must I endure days of conjecture before every match? We don't seem to be able to wait for anything anymore. Perhaps we have to take out our celebration in advance or mitigate our feelings of dejection in preparation in case the result is not the one we would wish. The other side of the coin is that after a victory, almost everything has been said in advance. There is little remaining to savour and enjoy.

Perhaps the age of the credit card has hastened the arrival of future events. We don't have to save any longer, we bung it on the plastic. 'Buy now and pay later' is the *zeitgeist* in our society driven by hurry-sickness. In June 2005, the Capital One credit card company wrote to its cardholders to inform them that a rise in the interest rate from 4.9% to 15.9% is an "upgrade." Well, Capital One's profits would be upgraded at least. Also at issue here is the term 'credit card.' These cards do not give you credit, they only put you in debt. But I guess that *debt card* doesn't sound appealing from a marketing point of view. We live in an age where a company called McDonalds can call the places where it sells slabs of previously deep frozen 'meat' between two pieces of aerated wheat flour as 'restaurants.' Would you enter a restaurant only to find that you had to eat with your fingers from a greasy piece of paper and wash your food down with fizzy sugared water from a cardboard cup? Please, grammar fascists, is this not worthy of your attention? Would you eat from a pail? Consider KFC, previously known as Kentucky Fried Chicken before the brand makeover. You are encouraged to buy chicken and ribs in a family-sized 'bucket.' Oh dear!

Another misnomer is the 10-year passport. Many countries insist that you have six months left on your passport before entering. Does this mean that our passports are now valid for only 9½ years?

We should protest against racist language. The newspaper headline screamed: "Cops arrest 'pistol Arab.'" The article claimed: "The 29-year-old suspect, who was travelling on a Swedish passport, was arrested…One passenger, who refused to be named said: 'They had Swedish passports but they looked like Arabs.' Earlier a number of Brits on the 80-mile bus ride from Stockholm city to the remote airport became worried about the Muslims' behaviour." How did the Brits know that their fellow passengers were Muslims? Even if the religion of the people on the bus was known, why mention it? What was the behaviour that so worried the Brits? Was it the threatening way they dressed or was facial prejudice at work? Why make the assumption that the people who looked like Arabs had false passports? Is it because Swedes are all blonde and blue-eyed (they most certainly are not) or that whatever this suspect looked like, it was obvious that he was not People Like Us. I won't shame the newspaper, but I think you might be able to guess which it is. Instead of worrying about trochees and spondees, write indignant letters to the editor of the unworthy rag in question in favour of more balanced reporting. If this sounds more like a complaint against racism than a discussion of language I offer no apology. Racism is objectionable. The case that I chose to highlight could have been written in a completely different way. There was no reason to resort to stereotyping and much of the article was pure speculation. Language can be manipulated by the unscrupulous and we need to always be on guard.

So, grammar fascists and others, I hope that this section has given you some food-for-thought about how we can act to tidy up English in a constructive way and therefore improve our lives just a little.

19. Won't get fooled again

If you believe everything you read, you better not read.

Japanese proverb

George Walker Bush, is renowned for his colourful use of English. "I made a wrong mistake" is one utterance attributed to him. Don't laugh. This is a deadly serious matter. For it just so happens that he is absolutely right. A mistake is an error. But a mistake only has relevance if two factors come into play. A mistake that nobody knows about or affects no-one has no significance. For example, my keyboard skills leave something to be desired. My first drafts are full of typing errors. However, few reach the public eye. I go over my work, check and change it. I also have a proof-reader who picks out the anomalies that I miss. So my typing mistakes don't matter as they are cleared up before thay cum owt. The second factor is if people in general regard what has been written or said as a mistake. It is the voice of the masses that decides whether it is a mistake or not. But what if the masses have been misled by people who should know better? What if matters of taste and style are judged absolutely by some unbreakable code. What if those that will judge are self-appointed and themselves decide the rules?

Grammar fascists loved Mrs Thatcher. Not always politically perhaps, but it was indeed she who uttered those immortal words: "There are no alternatives." What she meant is that any competing ideas of how to run the country to those of her own were incorrect and invalid. But she was right, pedantically at least. *Alternative* is derived from Latin *alter* means *second* as in alternate, meaning every other. Therefore, strictly speaking, there can only be one alternative. Should there be three things in question then they would be options. We should not only look for an alternative but seek options in the treasure chest of English.

Alternative is a keyword when it comes to English. Because when politicians promise, advertisements promote and regulations direct, we should be aware that an alternative meaning is often possible. There was a time when an asterisk was a mark that indicated a footnote. Although it can now be used to emote *author sighs*, an asterisk now has another purpose. It can be used to mean: 'The preceding statement is not true.' An advertisement offers: 'The quickest way to learn English. Guaranteed*' The asterisk will then point to the terms and conditions that say that you can get your money back with no questions asked. However, there is no information about how the company can demonstrate that it has the quickest method. It is not possible to prove the statement objectively. Therefore a guarantee cannot be given. There are lies, damned lies and asterisks

I was determined at the outset that *Eats, Roots & Leaves* should have no strong message. I did not want to fall into the same habits as the grammar fascists. I have tried not to judge except against those who attempt to sit in judgement. My only intolerance was to be against intolerance. Other than to highlight certain aspects of language, the only aim was to enjoy English. But it has become obvious to me that I have been trying to get a message across. We all own the English language and we have the right to use it as we see fit. To use it properly we need to exercise care and value judgements. We have to make sure that it doesn't fall under the control of others so that we unquestionably follow rules that others set.

Remember Jerry Leibowitz, the man who copyrighted the term quat-row in chapter 14? He isn't included in this rant. Not because he isn't a big corporation, but because he has the intellect, wit and business acumen to truly invent something new that wasn't in the public domain. And good luck to him. He was probably inspired by former Lakers coach Pat Riley. He owns the patent on the phrase "three-peat." It has been estimated that he has reaped more than $775,000 in licensing fees from t-shirts and jackets, including the one that I took a picture of in LA. Mr Liebowitz though did not reap the financial rewards he might have expected because the Lakers basketball team could not quite manage that fourth straight victory. Quat-row remains on the shelf waiting for a four-time commercial opportunity. While he is waiting, why not have a go at inventing your own phrase for five-in-a-row. It might at least be of interest to Robert Robinson and the Brain of Britain production team. Oh, and if you want the royalties, don't forget to register it. There are those who would steal the language from under our noses. Symbols such as © ® and ™ are placed after everyday words, names and phrases. This is where multi-national corporations try to steal English by patenting and reserving for their own benefit what belongs to all of us. I, for one, am not lovin' it and urge everyone to resist the McDonaldisation and Coca-Colonialism of English.

Google used to be a great tool for finding information on the internet. *The American Dialect Society* voted the neologism *to google* as the most useful word of 2002. However, Google's lawyers sent a cease-and-desist letter to a language website, demanding the removal of *google* as a verb from the dictionary. The letter included: "This definition implies that "google" [sic] is a verb synonymous with "search." Please note that Google is a trademark of Google Technology Inc. We ask that you help us to protect our brand by deleting the definition of "google" or revising it to take into account the trademark status of Google." You cannot claim copyright over a verb. Google, as a large company, is trying to use its corporate muscle to steal the language. You would have thought that the company should be pleased that people all over the world say to google. Like *h*oover, *biro* and many others, personal or trade names have become the generic name for a product or service. Can I be sued for saying that I am going to hoover the carpet this afternoon? This is exactly what I meant by others seeking control over English. It would be just as bad to let Microsoft decide how we write, by becoming too reliant on their software to check our spelling and grammar. Microsoftisation is rampant. The evidence is the predominant use of *color* instead of *colour* and *program* instead of *programme* when it comes to computer language. The following poem shows the danger of thinking that computers can sort out our mistakes.

Ode To The Spelling Checker

Eye halve a spelling chequer,
It came with my pea sea.
It plainly marques four my revue
Miss steaks eye kin knot sea.

Eye strike a quay and type a word
And weight four it two say
Weather eye am wrong oar write,
It shows me strait a weigh.

As soon as a mist ache is maid,
It nose bee fore two long,
And eye can put the error rite,
Its rare lea ever wrong.

Eye have run this poem threw it,
I am shore your pleased two no,
Its letter perfect awl the weigh,
My chequer tolled me sew.

A non knee mouse

A spell checker can only be effective when we know how to spell for ourselves. When a word appears on screen, the computer is programmed to assume that we had the right intention, but that we simply put a letter or two in the wrong place. All the spell-checker can do is to search its internal dictionary for words which are related to the misspelling that appeared on the screen. However, the computer cannot guess or imagine anything. The only thoughts represented are the intentions of the software designers. You still have to know how to spell to be able to choose from the list of options that the spellchecker presents. As the *Ode To The Spelling Checker* clearly demonstrates, the myriad[1] of homophones in English does not make computer spelling-checkers completely reliable. The computer cannot tell us that we have made a mistake if we have written a word that is spelled correctly, but is the wrong one.

Error-free composition is not the same as good writing. Anyone with a computer can produce something that has no grammatical or spelling faults. But that doesn't mean that the result will make sense or be interesting.

A great resource for anyone seeking information is the internet. However, the internet is democratic. Anyone can start up a website, get it noticed by the search engines and start spreading misinformation by accident or design. How can we be sure that the information provided is trustworthy? When it comes to language, there are any number of websites that are both reliable and correct. There are others which are much less so.

At first glance, you would instinctively trust a website belonging to The Department of Applied Linguistics & ESL at Georgia State University in Atlanta, USA. You google search 'British-American English.' Eighth on the list of websites is one called *"Common words in British and American English."* You scroll down the page and click on *Susan Jones' American vs. British Spelling Differences.*

---

[1]myriad can mean 10,000. It originates from the Greek *mýriās*. I intend the meaning of 'an indefinitely great number' as I don't know exactly how many homophones there are in English. I have heard talk of around 2,000.

Via an extra click, this leads to a page of tables that show the general principles of the differences between the two varieties of English. There is one table, for example, headed: " -or vs. -our." It shows, quite correctly, how Britons spell *honour* and Americans *honor*. The tables are so designed that we can assume that any British word ending in -*our* (labour, harbour) will end –*or* in American (labor, harbor). There is, however, a table with the title: "-ck or -k vs. -que."

The first line says that the American *check* is spelt *cheque* in Britain. So far, so good. The next line says that the American *checker* becomes *chequer* in British English. This is true, but only in the sense of a pattern of squares. Someone who checks checks in the USA would not be a cheque chequer in the UK. The third and final line informs us that a *bank* in America would be a *banque* in Britain. It could be joke. GSU might be the equivalent of the fictitious Bob Jones University (as opposed to the real one). Susan Jones may well be Bob's niece and having a laugh at us all. Serious or not, there may be many people who are taken in by this and think that this is indeed the correct British spelling. If the information was a well-intended mistake it demonstrates a shameful lack of fact chequing. It also shows the danger of taking one or two instances and making a rule from them.

Professor Robert Wilensky wrote: "We've all heard that a million monkeys banging on a million typewriters will eventually reproduce the entire works of Shakespeare. Now, thanks to the Internet, we know this is not true."

It isn't just the world wide web that may be inaccurate regarding English. While in the USA, I spent time in bookshops looking for works about American English. I found that I had to look for information backwards as there were plenty of books about British English and the comparative differences. I found many of them committing mistakes such as Susan Jones. The most oft repeated one was listing the US word *handcuffs* as *darbies* in British English. I had not encountered the word before entering my first New York bookshop and I asked countless people on my return if they had. I even asked a couple of police. I found no knowledge of it, even when prompted. The word does exist, or should I say did. It belongs to the large category of obsolete words that no-one uses anymore. As a bit of fun, I took a pile of Am-Brit dictionaries to the counter at a large *Borders* bookstore outside of Boston. I said that they had been placed in the wrong section. I had found them in reference, but they should be in fiction.

This chapter is meant to be a conclusion. I was taught that no new information should be introduced in a summary, but that the contents and arguments should be concisely presented. I have already ignored that advice. But now the end is near I shall attempt to sum up. While writing these concluding words, I was in Sweden checking my spelling and syntax. Taking a break, I read the following letter in *The Independent* under the heading: Watch your language.

Sir: Delivering his make-or-break
speech at the Labour Party
conference, Chancellor Gordon Brown
expressed the pious wish that
in future all immigrants to Britain
should be taught to speak proper
English. This from a man who had
just a couple of sentences previously
came out with the howler:
"My mother taught my brothers and I
..."
M H Whitestone
Buckfastleigh, Devon

I replied, alluding to previous correspondence
discussing ways to eat Marmite. *The Independent*
published my response just in the nick of time to be
included in this book:

Sir: M H Whitestone implies that
Gordon Brown saying "My mother
taught my brothers and I ..." is not
proper English. This is a matter of
preference similar to the choice of
whether to Marmite or not to Marmite.
I will judge Mr Brown on his policies
and actions. Please, no grammar
fascism here[1].
Nicholas Waters
Växjö, Sweden

Could I have a better ending? Yes, I could make a
summary.

[1] The letter was shortened by the editor.

English can be a confusing, contrary and confounding language. But its idiosyncrasies and inconsistencies should not be used as ammunition to fire at those who do not master the language in every way and in all contexts. We have the right to use English as we see fit. The language belongs to us all. We also have the right to be wrong. Forbearance should be exercised by those who do know better. Silence could be maintained by those who think they know better but don't. We have a duty to communicate clearly, but should show restraint and respect for those who do not manage to get their point across. Do not mock or ridicule. Avoid criticism for its own sake. Instead try to help and show understanding. Only be intolerant of intolerance.

20. Why *Eats, Roots & Leaves*?

On the 21st of March 2001, we were driving along the New South Wales coast road to Sydney in Australia. It had been raining heavily since we left Newcastle. There were no cats or dogs, but it had rained harder than I had seen in any film or television depiction of the land down under. The Australian tourist board does a good job of selling us sunshine. About 3 o'clock in the afternoon the sky cleared and bright autumn sunshine gave us the opportunity to escape the car for a break.

We turned into one of a number of small coastal resorts that pepper this part of the NSW coastline. We parked and strolled around. I didn't make a note of the name of this place at the time, but I am reasonably sure that it was Swansea. There was a record shop that was playing comedy through the speakers outside of the store. I browsed the racks of CDs as I listened to a very funny Australian and feminist comedian spit out a highly original routine about men. As I listened, I spotted a CD bearing the legend "May contain traces of nuts." I was down under gathering authentic material for a book to be called *Different Englishes*. As I had collected some strange examples, I thought that the nutty statement would be a better title for the book about English usage. I wrote it down on a scrap of paper. On my return to the northern hemisphere, the book became perpetually postponed by the need to earn a living. I waited so long to write the book that someone beat me to it and used the title.

While listening outside the CD store, I also noted down one of the jokes that I heard.

"Why is an Australian man like a koala bear? Because he eats, roots and leaves[1]."

There is no punctuation in speech and the meaning therefore is ambiguous. Whatever the diet of the koala, this woman had a viewpoint that Australian men are only interested in food and sex. The joke doesn't work if you try to include beer.

The problem with commas is that they put doubt into people's minds. There is a children's joke that sums up the comma and potential double meanings: "Would you rather an elephant attacked you, or a gorilla?"

In Sweden, where I give courses on the English language, I am continually asked by teachers of English about the differences between what is written in grammar books and the realities of everyday usage. The teachers are acutely aware that television and radio, newspapers and novels use English at variance with what they were taught. The utterances of their students, in contact with the wider world of English through pop music and the internet, prove a great diversity from what they had learnt. Standard texts do not provide all the answers.

Three years previous to the Australia trip, I had started using the term 'grammar fascists' to describe those people who didn't seem able to accept change in language. There are some quite glaring discrepancies between what language purists advocate and the English that is written and spoken by real people. I have also been asked with increasing regularity if I have written a book on the subject. Now I can simply pull out a copy of the book with the title that I borrowed[2] from a comedian in Australia.

The book should have been called *Eats, Roots and Leaves*. That was until I met Steve, the graphics designer who turned my hand-drawn sketch for the book cover into a computer image. He said the title should be changed. He pointed out that *and* destroyed the symmetry on the front. The book therefore became *Eats, Roots & Leaves*. Maybe the comedian meant an ampersand when she told the joke. Who knows?

[1] Root in Australian English is a euphemism for sexual activity.
[2] Actually I haven't borrowed the title. I have stolen it as I have no intention of giving it back.

Thank yous

Birgitta, Caroline, Mum, Dad and everyone else that knows me. Also, anyone did something that was good or kind. You know who you are.

References

Most of the sources of quotations and factual references have been omitted. *Eats, Roots & Leaves* is not meant as a work of reference. Too many footnotes and appendices cause clutter. I have this information successfully saved on my computer[1]. If you require any information please take contact by visiting **www.eatsrootsandleaves.co.uk**

---

[1]Isn't the over-use of *successfully* just so annoying? Do we need messages like this one? 'You have successfully completed your booking.' If the booking was not made, then we do not get a message saying that the booking has failed. If the booking was made, then there is no need to put *successfully*. The word *completed* is sufficient. Then there is the superfluous *different*. 'I speak 5 different languages.' Well, it wouldn't be much use if one spoke 5 languages and they were all the same, would it? Oh, and what about *absolutely*? Nowadays, it seems, whenever someone is in agreement rather than simply saying '*yes*,' the reply is a resolute '*absolutely*.' And another thing...